The Journey Home,
Daily Devotions with Swami Kripalu

John Mundahl

1

Disclaimer

Every time I used a picture off the Internet I tried to find if there were copyright restrictions on the picture. As there are millions of pictures on the Internet, this was, at times, tedious and difficult. To the best of my knowledge, there are no copyright restrictions on the pictures that I used for this book. If I made a mistake, it was unintentional. Please contact me and I will remove the picture.

Dedicated with love to the memory of
Swami Kripalu, Bapuji,
1913-1981

dreamatico.com

3

Introduction

Swami Kripalu, or Bapuji, as we called him, was one of India's greatest saints. He was born in India on January 13th, 1913, in the western state of Gujarat. We know little about him, as he spent most of his adult life in silence and never wrote an autobiography. *"The great saints in ancient India wrote about God, not themselves,"* he said, and he was no exception.

We do know that his father died when Kripalu was a boy and the family was thrown into poverty. When Kripalu was 19, he was saved from suicide by a mysterious old man who became his guru and guided him on his yogic ascent. The story of his stunning life which followed is told in my three books, "From the Heart of the Lotus, the Teaching Stories of Swami Kripalu," "A Sunrise of Joy, the Lost Darshans of Swami Kripalu," and, "The Swami Kripalu Reader, Selected Works from a Yogic Master." Serious students of Swami Kripalu should first read, "A Sunrise of Joy."

Great Saints and Masters, such as Kripalu, continue to inspire us long after they are gone, and that is the purpose of this book. A daily devotional practice focused on the life of a saint, combined with prayer, brings strength to our lives, and surely the life and teachings of Swami Kripalu can be used in this way.

Once again, I am grateful to Umesh Eric Baldwin for sharing pictures of Swami Kripalu for this book.

Hari Om Shanti, Shanti, Shanti. May there be peace everywhere.

John Mundahl, 2016

Steadfast a lamp burns sheltered from the wind. Such is the likeness of the yogi's mind, shut from sense-storms and burning bright to heaven.

When mind burns placid, soothed with holy wont, when Self contemplates self and in itself hath comfort, when it knows the nameless joy beyond all scope of sense, revealed to soul, only to Soul!

And knowing, wavers not, true to the farther Truth, when holding this it deems no other treasure comparable, but harbored there cannot be stirred or shook by any gravest grief---call that state "peace," that happy severance Yoga, and call that man the perfect Yogin!

Bhagavad Gita

Photo by Umesh Eric Baldwin. Summer, 1977. At the original Kripalu Yoga Retreat in Summit Station, Pennsylvania

"The spiritual path that I teach is called Sanatan Dharma, the Immortal Religion, or the path of Eternal Truth. Only Truth is eternal. Everything else is transitory and perishable. Although the word 'dharma' is often translated as 'religion,' in the phrase Sanatan Dharma it doesn't mean religion in the conventional sense of denomination, sect or creed. It means the performance of actions that lead to the attainment of Supreme Truth, which we often call God. Sanatan Dharma was first practiced by the rishis of ancient India. It is the experimentally proven Truth. This Truth has been realized and experienced by the great saints of all times in their meditations and through divine revelation. Truth doesn't belong to one race, creed, or country. It doesn't know such narrow distinctions. Truth is available to the entire world." *Swami Kripalu*

Bapuji writing on his slate in India. 1973. Photo by Umesh Eric Baldwin.

7

January

January 1st
(A New Year's Blessing)

The New Year is coming closer with a slow step. It's coming slowly, so you can make yourself new. The Indian New Year is a social celebration, but your New Year is a religious celebration because it includes the birth of a great Master. Holy Christ, the incarnation of love, gave two basic principles to the world: Love and Service. Love is God and Service is our puja, or worship to Him. All other principles are included in these two. You need not find love outside yourself. That love is already hidden in your heart. You only have to awaken it and radiate its light outward. May the New Year bring you happiness. May your humanitarian qualities increase. May the flower of your love bloom and may its fragrance spread everywhere. This is my blessing and good wishes to you. Your Beloved Grandfather, Bapuji. Jai Bhagwan.

Bapuji's hand.
Photo from archives
of Umesh Eric
Baldwin.

8

January 2nd
(A Blessing is Like a Pearl)

Well-wishing and a blessing may appear to be the same, but they aren't. Well-wishing comes from the surface of the mind, but a blessing comes from the depth of the heart. Well-wishing is like a bubble. A blessing is like a pearl. A stone can be thrown in many ways, weakly with our bare hand, or powerfully with a slingshot or a catapult. The momentum of each varies as the stone travels. Good wishes are like stones thrown by a weak arm, but blessings are like stones shot from a catapult. Those potent blessings generate faith and determination in the recipient and are never given in vain.

January 3rd
(Is God Really Everywhere?)

Often the great saints say, "God is everywhere!" But if God is everywhere, why can't we see Him? We have eyes. Why can't we see God if He's everywhere, then? This is an unusual situation. It's like a fish swimming in the ocean and yet asking, "Oh, Great Water, where are you?" There are two reasons for not finding something: One reason is that we've forgotten where we placed it. The other reason is that even though the thing is right in front of us, we don't have the ability to see it. Yes, God is everywhere, but we can't see Him because our eyes are bad. We need glasses, the glasses of pure character. We must step firmly upon the spiritual path and develop pure character. Pure character will bring purity to our heart, mind, and body and then we will see God.

Notes to Myself

10

January 4th
(Am I Headed for This Shore or Not?)

Decisions should be made when we are calm. This is where willpower resides. Decisions made when we're excited, or weak and lethargic are short-lived. The motivation that inspires us to do what's good for us, isn't something we can borrow from others. It must come from within us. Borrowed inspiration is short-lived and persists only in the presence of the motivator. We each have this innate ability to inspire ourselves. The power of this inner inspiration is long-lived and motivates us continually along our chosen path. Obstacles may arise, but we overcome them. Genuine seekers are courageous warriors. They never take a step backwards. They are one-pointed: "Am I headed for this shore or not? What's my decision?" That's what they ask themselves every day.

Notes to Myself

11

In the United States, summer, 1977. Photo from archives of Umesh
Eric Baldwin.

January 5th
(When Devotion is Still a Little Girl)

When devotion is still a little girl, she regards the ways of attaining God as toys and plays with them. When she attains maturity, she regards the means of attaining God as her greatest wealth. Only then can she give birth to a child in the form of Knowledge. When Knowledge reaches youth, devotion gives birth to a second child named Asceticism. The elder brother, Knowledge, is fond of his younger brother, Ascetiscism, and loves his younger brother to distraction. He cannot bear a moment's separation from his younger brother. Once Asceticism attains maturity, the Lord comes forth. Upon seeing Knowledge, Asceticism, and Devotion, the Lord becomes crazy with love.

*www.
pinterest.com*

13

January 6th
(The Charity Loved by the Lord)

The Lord secretly nourishes the sun and the moon with light. He secretly fills the earth with food. He secretly fills the clouds with water. Yes, we can clearly see the sun, the moon, the light, the earth, the food, the clouds, and the water, but our eyes cannot see the Lord, or any part of His body, or even His shadow. The Creator of the world is so great that He works in silence. Since we are His children, shouldn't our nature contain a bit of His charity? The charity loved by the Lord has two wings: Give Secretly, and, Give and Forget. That is, as much as possible we should give without others knowing. Pure charity is only that which we give with compassion and religious feeling. When a devotee offers pure charity with faith to God, God feels tremendously content and merges with the devotee, and makes him or her, his own.

Notes to Myself

January 7th
(Dada, I Love You)

Today one of my grand-daughters from India came to me and said, "Dada, I love you." She spoke to me in Gujarati. Her face was filled with love. Her eyes streamed love. Love radiated from her heart. Her words weren't necessary. Everything was evident. In the springtime, do blossoms have to say to the trees, "We love you?" When love comes straight from the heart, it's like poetry.

www.pinterest.com

January 8th
(True Love is for Fools)

Usually what we call love isn't love. True love never ends. Once the flame of true love is lit, it can never be put out. It doesn't start and stop, sometimes on, sometimes off. It's always giving and serving, no matter what. This is it's nature. One who cannot tolerate pain cannot travel on the path of true love. True love is for fools. They are fools to the desires of the world, so worldly people call them fools. But they aren't fools, really. They're simply full of love. Close your eyes and draw all your senses inward and enter the depth of your heart and ask yourself: Have I ever experienced this kind of love from anybody? It's so rare.

www.awesomelycute.com

16

January 9th
(There is Such Unusual Power in Love)

There is such unusual power in love. When we express this love for God, we are also loving our family, our community, and our nation. Our life becomes full of joy and loving others becomes our nature. If we want to be happy, we must give this happiness to others. God is clever. He has planned things in such a way that our happiness is locked within others, and their happiness is locked within ourselves. The key that opens that lock is love. Love comes from the heart and it opens the heart of the other.

petcoupon.wordpress.com

17

January 10th
((Lord, Cast Your Sweet Gaze on Me)

Sometimes only God can remove our faults. We're too weak on our own. Then we should pray to Him: *"My Lord, You're the destroyer of all the demons. Let Your grace fall upon me. Hold my hand and take me to Your lotus feet."*

Once a saint came to a town in India.

"My brothers and sister," he said. "Anger is a demon. Don't be angry with each other. When this demon enters your mind, it creates pain and suffering in others. Give up your anger."

A man was in the audience and he was moved by this discourse.

"I'll give up anger!" He said to himself with great conviction. "I will do this!"

He walked up to the saint afterwards and said,

"Your message went deep into my heart. I won't be angry anymore!"

The saint wasn't impressed. He knew such a vow was impossible and yet he didn't want to discourage the man, either. So he gently raised his hand and blessed the man.

"Yes, but do it gradually," the saint said. "Little by little, let go of your anger."

"What do you mean?" The man said. "Why should I do it slowly? I'll just push it out and be rid of it!"

"Yes, do that, then," the saint said, remaining calm. "Just push it out and be rid of it."

"I will!" the man said. "I'm finished with anger!"

18

The man left and went home.

When he got home his wife had left a bowl of milk in the middle of the floor and the man stepped on it by mistake and spilled it. Immediately, he got angry.

"Where are you?" He shouted to his wife.

His wife came running into the room and saw the spilled milk.

"Why did you leave this milk here?" The man demanded.

"I was getting some milk and the baby fell out of the crib," she said. "She cried, so I left the milk right there and ran to take care of the baby."

Now the man felt ashamed.

"I just promised that saint I wouldn't be angry anymore," he said, "And here I am angry already. And over nothing, too."

So he repeated his vow all over again, with even greater conviction:

"Anger is a demon! I won't be angry anymore!"

Then he thought, "Now, how can I remember that? I know. I'll make a sign."

So he made a sign for himself with big letters that said:

One Should Not Be Angry. Anger Is A Demon.

He wrote the words on a board and put the board on his desk at work. Now he was happy.

But later that day he started arguing with someone at work and he got so angry he hit the man with the board.

Sometimes only God can remove our faults and we should pray to Him: *"My Lord, cast your sweet gaze*

upon me. Come and take your seat upon the throne of my heart and smile and remove all my pains.
(From: "From the Heart of the Lotus, the Teaching Stories of Swami Kripalu," by John Mundahl, Monkfish Books, Rhinebeck, NY 2008.)

Bapuji in India. 1973. Photo by Umesh Eric Baldwin

January 11th
(Rest at the Feet of the Lord)

Pray to the Lord daily. Accept happiness and unhappiness as the grace of the Lord. The Lord keeps the sun in the sky so everyone can have heat and light, and keeps the moon in the sky so everyone can have coolness at night. The Lord opens the flowers and allows them to bloom, and then closes and dries them up. All of these things happen by the will of the Lord and we are His children and He loves us. He doesn't want us to suffer or to be anxious. So rest, rest at His holy feet knowing you are cared for.

My prayer for the day is…

yourdailygerman.com

January 12th
(All Answers Lie With Love)

Wherever a lamp goes, it sheds its light. Wherever a flower goes, it sheds its fragrance. So also devotees of the Lord spread their love wherever they go. Try to live your life like that. Just love. Wherever you go, just spread your love. Just keep your candle of love going. Whenever you find a candle unlit, light it up, get it going, everywhere. There's no other way than that. Remember this principle. Hold on to this principle. All answers lie with love. Suffering is all that's left after losing love.

Photo from archives of Umesh Eric Baldwin. Sumner, 1977.

January 13th
(The Angle of Struggle)

Today you have gathered to celebrate my birthday. It is the start of my 67th year and I bless you with all my heart. I'm an old sadhak wanting only final liberation. You call me Dada, or Grandfather, and it isn't proper for me to cry in front of you, but every word I speak, every gaze from my eyes, is full of love for you. I don't speak English, but can any language truly express love? No, love is expressed only through the heart and the eyes.

Life is the flow of our own existence between birth and death. Some people say that life is an endless circle of mistakes that can never be prevented, or that life is a chaotic mixture of happiness and unhappiness. Other people take a different view. They say that life means love. Life means progress. Life means light. Life means evolution. Both groups agree, however, that life means struggle, that we all must struggle. This world is a battlefield. Anyone born has to be a warrior, whether you are boy or girl, man or woman, young or old, king or beggar, literate or illiterate, saint or sinner, our major dharma or duty in this world is to fight.

The compassionate Lord has one special Angel to help with our fight. This is the Angel of Struggle.Just as our food won't digest properly without exercise, so too our life won't develop properly without struggle. The outward form of struggle may appear cruel, but its inner nature is not malicious. She enters our life without invitation and does whatever she pleases, but she blesses us with true knowledge, the knowledge we each need at that moment in our life. How skillful she is! What a beautiful sculptor!

Bapuji in India. 1973. Photo by Umesh Eric Baldwin.

24

January 14th
(The Middle Way)

Once Lord Buddha conducted an experiment in diet. He began by taking a handful of rice and counting the grains. He then decreased the number of grains he ate each day by one grain. Eventually only one grain remained so he only ate one grain of rice that day. However, one day he fell unconscious from weakness. On that day he decided to take the middle path saying, "If the strings of an instrument are kept too loose, they cannot produce music, and if they are kept too tight they will break. An instrument can only give music when tuned the middle way, neither too loose nor too tight." Similarly, we should live by the middle way, neither too much nor too little of anything.

www.123rf.com

January 15th
(The Light of Renunciation)

The light of renunciation can be lit and it can also be put out. So that this light may not be put out, you have to stay awake for all of your life. As soon as you fall asleep, as soon as you lose your wakefulness, the light will be turned off. This Divine Light is the life. As long as you have not arrived at the Divine lotus feet of the Lord, you have to keep up your pilgrimage, your journey to the Divine. You must not be tired. You must be patient. Don't lose your enthusiasm or become weak. This light is the light of the Divine knowledge. It is the light of love and the light of tapas (discipline). One who holds this Divine light has their Guru and the Lord in their heart. Become that light and continually remain burning. This burning is the sadhana (spiritual practice). It is the tapas. I pray to the Lord that our journey together may reach to the gate of the Lord. The Lord is the leader of us all. He is the one who is taking us from untruth to truth, from darkness to light, from death to immortality. At his feet we bow down millions and millions of times. You have my blessings. Your beloved Dada, Bapuji.

Today my prayer is…

January 16th
(A Child and Her Doll)

Sanatan Dharma, the eternal religion of India, allows devotees to worship whatever form or aspect of God that is most meaningful to them. So India is full of statues. Isn't this idol worship? How can there be life in stone? Have you ever watched a child play with a doll? She treats the doll as if the doll were alive. She talks to the doll and feeds and dresses the doll and comforts the doll when the doll cries. For her the doll is alive. In a similar manner, for the people of India, their chosen form of God is alive, too, and they worship that form daily in a ceremony called, puja. Their chosen form of God isn't just a statue of stone. The statue opens their heart and their devotion becomes a form of meditation and it purifies their mind.

www.encouraging.com

27

January 17th
(One Sun in the Sky is Enough)

The spiritual history of India is so great that it's almost beyond description. Even now, in India's sad state, there are still samskaras, or impressions, from this past glory. One of these customs is that a person may adopt the clothes of a swami and be taken care of by society. Today in India there are hundreds of thousands of sadhus and they are all fed, clothed, and housed by Indian society, even by the poorest of the poor. Naturally, some abuse this system. But India believes that saints are the gems of the country and just as it takes tons of coal to produce one diamond, it takes tons of sadhus to produce one true saint. India believes this is worthwhile. One sun in the sky is enough. It is enough for the entire world.

Shaivite sadhu,
Kedarnath Shiva Temple,
Garhwal Himalaya,
North India. Photo by
Umesh Eric Baldwin

28

January 18th
(The Guru's House)

For spiritual progress you must take up your abode in an ashram every now and then and do spiritual practices. The Guru's house is your house. It is the abode of peace and happiness, the school of abstinence and the pilgrimage of knowledge. It is the house of the Lord. Only a lit lamp can light an unlit lamp. The guru is the lit lamp and the disciple is the unlit lamp. Even if we study the scriptures, we cannot comprehend certain portions of the scriptures through our rational mind alone. We need the help of the Guru. The lineage of sacred knowledge continues in this way.

www.pinterest.com

January 19th
(Those Who Suffer for the Pain of Others)

The pain of others doesn't touch everyone. Those touched by the pain of others are God's messengers because God can comfort his suffering children through them. We are all suffering. We all have our pains to bear, but those who suffer for the pain of others are especially loved by God. Just think, we can all become great philanthropists. We can all give comfort to the hearts of others by giving a loving glance to someone in despair. This is compassion and it is born when we feel the pain of others. It is the daughter of non-violence and the religion of Love. It is the religion of everyone and the religion of the Lord.

www.atheismresource.com

Today my prayer is…

30

January 20th
(Where Can We Run To?)

The Lord is profoundly graceful and compassionate. He is eager to take us all in His arms. He waits for us patiently outside the doors of our heart. But we look away. We don't allow Him in. But where can we run to? Eventually we will have to turn to Him for shelter, comfort and support.

Mother and daughter, Gujarat, India. Photo by Umesh Eric Baldwin.

31

January 21st
(This is the Way to Grow)

The Lord is the giver of the fruits of our actions and He is just. He is always on the side of truth. By His will someone becomes a king, another a beggar. Someone is happy, another is sad. Someone is smiling, another is crying. Make good decisions with planning and proper understanding and then be satisfied and forget about it. Whatever the Lord does is always in the best interests of everyone. Accept happiness and unhappiness as the grace of God. This is the way to grow.

Photo from archives of Umesh Eric Baldwin. Winter, 1979.

32

January 22nd
(Shraddha)

Faith that cannot be disturbed or destroyed, even under trying conditions, is called *shraddha* in the scriptures. It means powerful faith that cannot be extinguished. It is generated in the heart and converts a stone or a man into a deity. It makes possible the attainment of good conduct, restraint, love, simplicity, firm determination and devotion to duty. This is the miracle of faith. It has divine power. Such faith has been a source of strength for extraordinary people who performed great tasks. Exhibiting divine patience, faith and devotion to their work, such powerful people have lived in the past, are living in the present and will live in the future. This is the flame that we should keep burning in our hearts.

thebluetemple.wordpress.com

33

January 23rd
(The Pauper's Treasure)

Those with wealth are considered rich. Yet, if they are not generous, they are paupers, because they are behaving like paupers. Conversely, those who are poor, but generous, are wealthy, because they are behaving like wealthy people. Someone who gives to others according to their capacity is truly a wealthy, cultured person.

Two young Tibetan girls, Lhasa Tibet. Photo by Umesh Eric Baldwin.

January 24th
(The Empty Bowl)

Humility is the landmark of knowledge and pride is the landmark of ignorance. Without humility, it is impossible to receive knowledge. If a cup full of milk is placed above an empty bowl, the milk will flow into the bowl. However, if the empty bowl is on top of the cup, no milk will flow into it. In the same manner, an egotistical disciple cannot receive knowledge from a Guru. The idea that if one bows down he is insignificant and if one doesn't bow down he is great, is false. The branches of a tree laden with fruit bow low. An older person bends down to pick up a child.

kingorchard.com

35

January 25th
(Spiritual Thirst)

There may be 25 pots of water on a table, but if you're not thirsty, what good are the pots? Likewise, if you're not thirsty for spiritual growth, what good is the Guru who is a pot of divine knowledge? So, first we must be thirsty. Then we must prepare ourselves to receive the teachings. What good is an expensive musical instrument in the hands of a child?

Bapuji as a young man in India. Photo from archives of Umesh Eric Baldwin.

January 26th
(They Give Us Peace)

High saints are the wealth of any nation. They do not think about themselves. They think about the happiness of others. It is difficult to recognize them. You will have to be around them for a long time. But there is one sure sign of their sainthood: They give us peace.

Photo from archives of Umesh Eric Baldwin. Winter, 1979.

January 27th
(When We Love Another)

Great souls love everyone in the world, but we must start by loving those we can. When a husband puts his eyes in front of his wife like two cannons, love seeks the first open door and escapes. It is the same for a wife, if she acts that way. Love is a form of God. When we love another, God is born in our heart.

The young and the aged . Sherpa ladies, Nepal. Photo by Umesh EricBaldwin.

38

January 28th
(Love is the Highest Mantra)

Love is God. It is the highest mantra. Start with your family and love them as yourself. Consider their happiness your greatest happiness. Give them so much love they cannot be without you. They should feel your absence. Their hearts should leap when they see you, such should be the depth of your love. To nourish this kind of love, you must continually burn like a lamp and for that you have to practice self-sacrifice.

pandawhale.com

January 29th
(When Working With Others)

W hen working with others for a noble cause, determine that you will love each other totally, that you will not hide from each other, or hurt or quarrel with each other. The grace of God will then flow into your work and give strength to what you do.

www.balipuribendesavillas.com

Notes to Myself

January 30th
(When You Bow to Me during Celebrations)

I feel the Beloved Lord showering love as He appears in your tear-filled eyes and hearts when you bow to me during celebrations. These festivals have made me a lover of God and a lover of disciples since for me, this scene is like the darshan of the Lord. Whatever I have said about the language of love and our relationship of love is due to my seeing the love in your eyes and feeling the tide of sentiment in your hearts. It is overwhelming. I cannot hold it.

Photo from archives of Umesh Eric Baldwin. Summer, 1977

January 31st
(Sahaj Yoga)

Our yoga is known as Sahaj Yoga (natural yoga), Sanatan Yoga (eternal yoga), Anugraha Yoga (yoga of grace), Saranagati Yoga (yoga of surrender), Atmasamarpana (yoga of self-sacrifice), Prema Yoga (yoga of love), Raja Yoga (royal yoga), Maha Yoga (great yoga), or Nirvikalpa Yoga (yoga of the dissolution of the mind.)

In Sahaj Yoga, the proficient master yogi awakens the vital power in his disciple with his blessings. This results in the involuntary performance of yogic kriyas (activities) in the disciple. He accepts that he doesn't do anything willfully and readily accepts the will of the Omnipresent.

This self-surrender doesn't bear with any argument. It is a thing to be experienced. Therefore, it isn't possible for the layman to understand the second-hand descriptions of this experience.

In this sadhana, prana slowly reaches the sex center. As soon as this happens, the conflict between prana and apana begins. This results in the awakening of sensual desires. In the beginning, the sadhak thinks this is a short disturbance that will subside in a few days. But as he progresses, sexual desire increases. He continues his practice for three or four years with full faith.

Then his faith starts wavering. He cannot understand what to do. His problem is solved only when he gets the guidance of an experienced master. Then he

42

is at peace with himself, after completely surrendering to his Guru.

Bapuji in India. Photo from archives of Umesh Eric Baldwin.

February

February 1st
(Open Your Heart to God)

First, make your personal life beautiful and pure. Imagine there are thousands of candles arranged in front of you in a circle, but the candles are not lit, so it gets dark at night. But in the middle of all the candles there is one burning and that is you, your ability to bring love into this world. And from that one candle you can light all the other candles so the darkness goes away. One candle can light thousands. This is what great saints do. They are clouds of God's love. Through them, those who are suffering find peace and joy. And you can do that, too. Open your heart to the love of God and see what happens.

Notes to Myself

February 2nd
(Faith is Power Itself)

The Lord teaches in the Shiva Samhita that faith is the first component of any accomplishment. Faith is power itself, the power of mantra, the power in a statue, the power of teacher and teachings. All of these work in proportion to your trust and faith. Whatever amount of faith you have, you will experience that amount of result. As soon as faith is generated in one's mind, progress becomes simple.

www.caclubindia.com

45

February 3rd
(The Prasad of the Lord)

To equate wealth with material abundance is false. Anything we consider valuable is an asset: Our time, our knowledge, our understanding, our ability to love, our ability to care for others. These are all forms of prosperity. Some portion of whatever we are capable of giving should be set aside for others. Only then should we wholeheartedly enjoy what remains. Charity, or giving, is a lotus flower. The enjoyment it brings to us becomes the Lord's prasad (blessed food).

tinybuddha.com
Notes to Myself

46

February 4th
(Pride Means Multiplication)

Wise men don't praise themselves. If others praise them, they are not carried away. Nor do they think of themselves as men of great wisdom. Pride means multiplication. That is, a proud person makes a show of being many more times virtuous than he really is. Humility means division. A humble person makes little of his virtues. A proud person is blind because he sees only himself. A humble person has divine sight, because he sees only others.

Photo from archives of Umesh Eric Baldwin. Fall, 1977, Kripalu Yoga Retreat, Summit Station, Pennsylvania.

February 5th
(The Flower and the Corpse)

High saints don't exhibit their virtues. Good men try to hide their virtues and bad men try to hide their vices. But neither virtue nor vice can be hidden. How can one conceal the perfume of flowers in a beautiful garden, or the putrid smell of a rotten corpse in a ditch? We should admit our faults and be rid of them. An individual who cannot do without praise is like a cripple who cannot walk without crutches.

Bapuji at his writing desk. 1978. Photo by Pandavi Anna Pool.

Today I am thankful for…

February 6th
(Love is the First Lesson)

L ove is the first lesson. Start by loving your family and everyone around you. Your loved ones will have faults, but don't throw them out of your life. If someone has a boil on their arm, you operate on the boil, but you don't cut their arm off.

www.sodahead.com

Today I choose to forgive….

February 7th
(The Ink of Love)

Thank you for this beautiful card. Your names are now on the card of my heart because you wrote your names with the pen of your eyes and the ink of love. This ink is special. It cannot be erased. So your names will be with me for many lifetimes. *(Bapuji, before leaving for Toronto, summer, 1977.)*

Notes to Myself

www.asingleroseflorist.com

50

February 8th
(True Love is Just an Offering)

True love is just an offering. It does not expect something in return. There is no hesitation in true love, because it does not expect anything back. That is the principle of love. It is a free will offering. It isn't an exchange. There's no begging. To enter the heart of another is to forget our ego. This is the offering. This is the surrender. It is the grand experiment of our existence. We are born to love each other. What a beautiful way to purify our ego.

www.
pinterest.
com

February 9th
(We Cannot Survive without Love)

A yogi can bring prana wherever he wants. In the same way, once we have love in our heart, we can bring love wherever we want. Nothing is higher than this. We can get rid of many possessions and still survive, but we cannot survive without love. They say when a person stops breathing that he's dead, but I don't think so. A person is dead when they have no love in their heart. They're part of the living dead.

www.upfyre.com

Notes to Myself

52

February 10th
((Isn't This Amazing!)

We read so many books, go to so many workshops and listen to so many talks on spiritual growth and yet we don't change. Isn't this amazing! The reason why this happens is because we don't have control over our minds yet, so we cannot apply what we have learned. By firmly practicing the yamas and niyamas, we begin to experience mental control and thus we progress spiritually.

www. pinterest. com

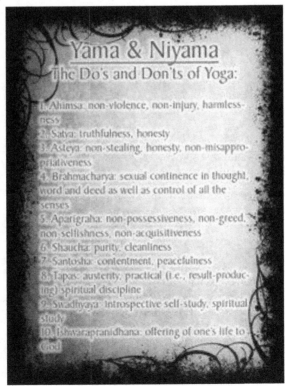

Yama & Niyama
The Do's and Don'ts of Yoga:

1. Ahimsa: non-violence, non-injury, harmless-ness
2. Satya: truthfulness, honesty
3. Asteya: non-stealing, honesty, non-misappro-priativeness
4. Brahmacharya: sexual continence in thought, word and deed as well as control of all the senses
5. Aparigraha: non-possessiveness, non-greed, non-selfishness, non-acquisitiveness
6. Shaucha: purity, cleanliness
7. Santosha: contentment, peacefulness
8. Tapas: austerity, practical (i.e., result-produc-ing) spiritual discipline
9. Swadhyaya: introspective self-study, spiritual study
10. Ishwarapranidhana: offering of one's life to God

February 11th
(The Supreme Way to Happiness)

In the same way that whiteness and liquidity are inseparable from milk, so, too, surrender and service are inseparable from love. This means that we should live for a beloved person, or for others, not for ourselves. This is the supreme and infallible way to achieve happiness. When we enter the heart of our beloved and allow our beloved into our heart, oneness occurs. This oneness is called love. Surrender and service to each other then become so subtle they are invisible.

Girl coveting her new found water bottle on a mountain pass in western Nepal. Photo by Umesh Eric Baldwin.

54

February 12th
(God is Love)

Almighty God is love. Surrender and Service are His two Holy feet, and His feet purify us all. We humbly pray to Almighty God that He be compassionate and purify us all.

Village lady in the Nepal Himalaya. Namaskar Mudra. Photo by Umesh Eric Baldwin.

My Prayer Today is…

February 13th
(The Place to Get Drowned)

Meditation is when you forget yourself. When you remember yourself, you experience duality: joy and sorrow, pleasure and pain, day and night. When you forget yourself, you merge with God. That is the place to get drowned.

Photo from "www.naturalmeditation.net."

February 14th
(The Birth of Attachment)

A few years after birth, we begin to recognize our own individual existence. The moment we begin to distinguish between yours and mine, attachment is born. In Sanskrit, the word is *parigraha*. It means *to store, to accumulate with strong attachment, to hold on to*. Non-attachment is a virtue because it creates a peaceful mind. A person practicing non-attachment cultivates voluntary simplicity and discharges his or her duties in life while remaining free of obsessive desires.

Is There Anything I Don't Need Anymore?

February 15th
(Simple Acts of Service)

When we begin our spiritual journey, we must start from a state of high attachment and gradually travel in the direction of nonattachment. We can practice sadhana only according to our capacity. Start by performing simple acts of service for others. Nonattachment grows whenever we perform selfless actions. When a school teacher solves a math problem on the blackboard, does she solve it for herself? No, she solves it for her students. Any action not motivated by selfish desire, performed for the love of God, is the best of all forms of non-attachment.

Photo from archives of Umesh Eric Baldwin.

February 16th
(Our Cries of Pain)

Many unhappy people come to the saints for help. How can I find peace, they ask? This question has been with us forever and ever. Our restless minds are the cause of the disturbance, and to bring our minds back to rest, we must firmly let go of disturbing thoughts. Just as a baby pulls his own hair and then cries, unaware that he is causing his own pain, so too we hold on to our destructive thoughts and then cry in pain.

www.focusforhealth.org

Notes to Myself

59

February 17th
(The Eternal Path Back to God)

The cause of unhappiness is separation from God. The cause of happiness is reunion with God. The nature and purpose of prayer, or remembrance, is reunion with God. Prayer is the first step of yoga. It is the silent speech of love. It is the light of love. It is the only eternal path back to God.

Photo from archives of Umesh Eric Baldwin. 1980.

My Prayer Today is…

60

February 18th
(Pray to the Divine Beings for Mercy)

B e patient. Love the Lord. Life is very, very difficult. We will inevitably make mistakes. Pray to the divine beings for mercy. "Lord, You are my entire life. You be my guard. Stay in my heart. Stay in my eyes. I have no other answer than this prayer: Merciful One, keep your merciful eyes upon me."

www.pinterest.com

My prayer today is…

61

February 19th
(A Saint Hurts My Feelings)

Once I went for the darshan of an old, famous Mahatma in India. He was traveling by train and I heard that his train was going to make a short stop in the town where I lived. He had many disciples in my town and they, too, wanted to see him.

I was a swami by then, but I was a young swami. The social custom in India is that saints should always be pleased to see each other, and the older saint should be garlanded by the younger saint.

The train stopped and Mahatma Guruji came out and stood in the doorway of the train car so everybody could have his darshan. Hundreds of people pressed close to see him. I applied sandalwood to his forehead and placed a garland around his neck and he smiled at me. Normally in India when an older saint greets a younger saint, the older saint will embrace the younger saint. He won't just smile; he'll take a special moment and embrace the younger saint. They do this to encourage the younger saint.

On this particular day, Mahatma Guruji just smiled at me. He smiled sweetly, but he didn't embrace me and I was a little bit hurt.

The train left and I returned to my residence. I thought deeply about what had happened. Then I realized that it was impossible for him to embrace me. There were hundreds of people pressing close for his blessing. Furthermore, he was standing two steps above me and he was much older than me and it would have

62

been difficult for him to bend over that far and embrace me without causing pain to his body.

So I realized *my expectation was incorrect, not the action of Mahatma Guruji*, and I became happy. I had figured out truly what had happened and I was no longer hurt.

The next day, to my great surprise, I received a visit. Mahatma Guruji=s main disciple came to see me. He was a wealthy landowner and he traveled with Mahatma Guruji to take care of his needs. He had come to my residence only to pay his respects to me.

"After our train left your town," he told me, "Gurudev talked about you and he praised you over and over and he sent me to see you. He loves you very much."

There is a phrase in India: *I recognized my mistake and I held my own hand. It means: I took responsibility for my own wrong thought or action.*

This is the essence of the story. This is what we should remember from this story.

I saw Mahatma Guruji one more time. Several years passed. Accidently he fell on the bank of the Nirmada River and hurt his leg badly. They brought him to Daboine for medical care. By chance, I was staying only 10 miles away. It was Guru Purnima, so he had his Guru Purnima in Daboine and I went for his darshan one more time before he died.

(From: "From the Heart of the Lotus, the Teaching Stories of Swami Kripalu," by John Mundahl. Monkfish Books, Rhinebeck, New York 2008)

ॐ

February 20th
(True Religion)

True religion is like a needle. It brings two pieces, two people, together. Non-religion is like a scissors. It divides and makes two out of one. True religion brings unity. It teaches love and togetherness. This is its basic purpose. It never puts a wall between us and others.

Village girl helping in the fields. Garhwal Himalaya, North India. Photo by Umesh Eric Baldwin

February 21st
(How Can We Recognize A Saint?)

If we touch a shaven head in the darkness, should we believe we've touched a saint? If we see long hair swaying on someone's shoulders during the daylight, should we believe we've seen a saint? How can we recognize a saint? Should we look for saffron clothes or tilak (sandalwood paste) on a person's forehead? No, a saint isn't recognized by his body, but by his temperament. What is in the mind of ordinary people isn't in their speech. And what is in their speech isn't in their conduct. But the thought, speech and conduct of a saint are harmoniously synchronized.

<u>Notes to myself</u>

Bapuji writing on his slate. Photo from archives of Umesh Eric
Baldwin. Summer, 1978.

February 22nd
(The Spiritual Mind)

The whole world is one family and we are all brothers and sisters. No matter what religion we are following, if we cannot love others we are not following religion, but the illusion of religion. Religion teaches the oneness of all. To see this requires a broad mind, the spiritual mind. The narrow mind focuses on our own self and is selfish.

Boy on a mountain trail in western Nepal. Photo by Umesh Eric Baldwin

February 23rd
(Service Makes One out of Two)

Service is the heavenly beauty of love, the sweetest fragrance of love, the bright light of love. Service makes one out of two. It is the love process that makes two hearts beat as one, two lives as one. Service is the youth of love. Through it the flower of love blooms. It purifies all.

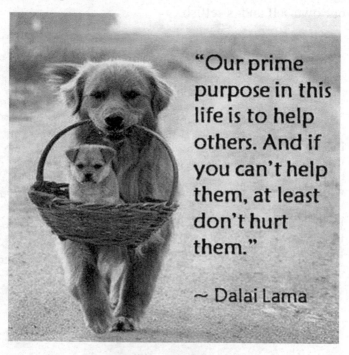

"Our prime purpose in this life is to help others. And if you can't help them, at least don't hurt them."

~ Dalai Lama

quotesgram.com

Today I will reach out to someone close to me and help them in some small simple way, and I won't tell anyone.

February 24th
(Look Upon Others with Gentle Eyes)

S hots from a gun or blows from a sword are dangerous, but violence from destructive speech is worse. The tongue is as strong as an elephant because it can crush someone. Speak sweetly without harming anyone and look upon others with gentle eyes.

www.flowersoxfordshire.co.uk

Notes to Myself

February 25th
(Speak the Truth, but do so Sweetly)

The headstand is a difficult posture, but purification of speech is more difficult than a thousand headstands. Yogically speaking, if we haven't learned to speak the truth, and to speak it sweetly, we haven't learned to speak. We can pronounce words and repeat sounds of the alphabet, but it isn't speech until we are speaking the truth and doing so sweetly. Try to keep silent for two hours a day. Then gradually increase it to one whole day. Pick a day, say Thursday, when you will practice doing this and try to remain alone. This will create heat or tapas. You do this intentionally. Observe your thought pattern while remaining silent.

Today, I will be conscious of my speech.

February 26st
(A Special Gift)

I have observed silence for 18 years. What benefit did I get from doing this? There are many benefits and it could be the topic of an entire talk, but I will tell you about one gem that I received. The gift is self-observation. Whenever I behave improperly during the day, it causes me suffering in my sadhana. Deep self-observation happens automatically during my sadhana and my mistake comes running to me. It just jumps out right in front of me, even though I may have completely overlooked it during the day. To me this is a wonderful grace, because this is how I grow. Without this special gift, my life would not be what it is today.

1978. Photo from archives of Umesh Eric Baldwin.

February 27th
(The Haughty Elephant)

God has given us a tongue so we can talk. However, it acts like a horse without a reign or a haughty elephant. Lord Krishna says in the Bhagavad Gita that if a devotee wants to feel devotion for God, he must triumph over his tongue and his genitals. Just as a dog wags his tail when he sees his owner, so our mind wags its tail at the command of these two organs.

Village dog in Gujarat, India. Photo by Umesh Eric Baldwin.

72

February 28th
(This World is a Battlefield)

This world is a battlefield. Everyone born has to be a warrior. Whether we are boy or girl, man or woman, young or old, king or beggar, brave or coward, literate or illiterate, saint or sinner, we have to fight the battle. Our major dharma, or duty, is to fight. Our struggle begins with birth and exists up to our last breath. Life can end, but the battle cannot.

Notes to Myself

March

March 1st
(Invoking the Lord in our Heart)

Everyone in the world can give generously, whether they are rich or poor. To equate charity solely with gifts of money, clothes or food is false. We can give gifts of education, security and comfort. The Lord is invoked in our heart whenever it melts at the sight of a helpless person's intolerable pain. At such times, our heart becomes illuminated with the Lord's divine light.

Today my thought is…

March 2nd
(Wherever there is Love, there is God)

There are many virtues, but the highest of all is love. Just as by lifting one flower of a garland, the whole garland is lifted, so also by lifting the flower of love, the whole garland of virtues comes to us. Wherever there is love, there is God. This is heaven.

Photo from: "www.naturalmeditation.net"

Notes to Myself

March 3rd
(Our Only Aim)

When our only aim is to attain the Supreme Being, non-attachment is accomplished spontaneously without effort. Just as a traveler heading west is naturally going away from the east, a seeker heading toward liberation is naturally moving away from worldly illusion. When seekers desiring liberation begin yoga sadhana, previous attachments remaining in their minds, however few, manifest and create disturbance. But the seeker frees himself from them through the power of discrimination, which increases daily as his mind and body purify. The more our love for the Lord increases, the more our love for worldly illusion decreases.

Bapuji in India. Photo from archives of Umesh Eric Baldwin.

March 4th
(From Attachment to Non-Attachment)

Non-attachment is one of the five goals of spiritual life. It means to not accumulate or hoard. We're born attached, so naturally we want to accumulate things. It's as difficult to move from attachment to non-attachment as it is to move from the earth to the sky. It simply can't be done in a single bound. Only a gradually step- by- step ascent is possible. If a thousand pounds of grain were piled in front of us do you think we could eat it all in a day? Of course not. But if we had a hundred years to live we could eat ten piles that big.

Chili peppers drying in the South Indian sun. Photo by Umesh Eric Baldwin.

March 5th
(The Tracks of Religion)

Imagine if a train decided that it didn't need tracks, that it would go wherever it wanted to? There would be an accident, of course. Likewise, if we give up the tracks of religion, we will have an accident, too. Don't let this happen to you. Stay awake and let your life be guided by the tracks of religion, even though it may be hard at times. The tracks of religion are the yamas and niyamas. These are the foundation of the spiritual life.

www.mindstreamyoga.com

March 6th
(Religion isn't in Books or Temples)

Religion isn't in books or temples. It lives within us. And the first lesson is love...that is, self-sacrifice...when we're willing, at least for a moment, to put the needs of others ahead of our own.

Photo from archives of Umesh Eric Baldwin. 1978.

March 7th
(A True Saint)

A small child doesn't become elderly if he wears the clothes of his grandfather, puts spectacles on his little nose and tries to walk and talk like him. Similarly, no person can become a saint simply by acting like a saint in external ways. We recognize the extent of his genuineness sooner or later. To do so, however, we must come in close contact with him and even then we may be unable to recognize a genuine saint if we don't know how to identify virtues.

Bapuji at his writing desk. Photo by Pandavi Ana Pool. 1978.

March 8th.
(A Bottle of Perfume)

We want peace, but we aren't willing to be silent. We speak much more than necessary. Our bitter words result in quarrels. When gentle people speak, it is like a bottle of perfume has opened. When arrogant people speak, it is like a foul-smelling sewer has opened. So when you speak, open a bottle of perfume, not a sewer.

Today I will be conscious of my speech.

March 9th
(The Two Feet of the Lord)

The great poets and Masters of India say, "Hold on to the feet of the Lord. Go to His feet. Hold on to those feet." But how can we hold on to the feet of the Lord? He doesn't have a body. The two feet of the Lord are: *Right Conduct and Self-Mastery.* Hold on to those feet and know that you have held the feet of the Lord.

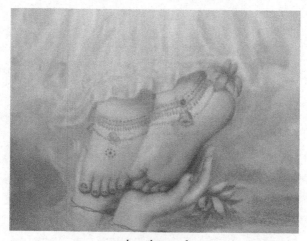

www.harekrsna.de

<u>Notes to Myself</u>

March 10th
(My First Meal as a Swami)

The saint who gave me swami initiation was Shantanandiji Maharaj. I was 32 years old at the time. With this initiation, I vowed to be detached from everything: my relatives, my home, my town, everything.

I left the ashram the next day and set out on my own. I now had to beg for food and be prepared to sleep under a tree wherever my feet stopped for the day. I had never asked for alms before and I was hesitant.

"How can I beg for food?" I asked myself. I felt helpless.

I walked three or four miles and came to a small town. There was a temple there and I went in, bowed to the altar, and sat in the corner of the temple. It was exactly twelve o'clock noon and time for a meal.

I wasn't particularly hungry and was thinking to myself,

"Maybe I'll go for two or three days before I ask for food. I can make it that long. But I'll certainly have to ask for alms after four or five days."

The women of India, the mothers and sisters, are so kind that as soon as a swami asks for alms they immediately give food, no matter how poor they are, so I wasn't too concerned about food.

As I sat in the corner of the temple, I noticed there was another temple behind it. Both temples were in the same compound close to each other and a mother and her son appeared to be living in the other temple. I could see that they did the pujas in both temples.

"Mother," I heard the boy say, "Yesterday, aunty promised that she would join us for our noon meal. But she's not coming now. She says that she's already eaten. What are we going to do with this extra food?"

"Oh," the mother said. "Don't worry about it. Go and finish your puja in the other temple."

The boy walked into the temple where I was sitting and he finished the puja with great devotion. Then he saw me and hurried back to his mother.

"Mother," he said. "There's a swami sitting in the other temple."

"My son," the mother said. "This extra food that we prepared today is for him. Go and tell him not to seek alms anywhere else, because his food is already prepared."

The son quickly came to me. He bowed down.

"Please come to our home for your noon meal," he said sweetly.

There are two types of alms for swamis in India. In the first one, the swami sits and eats with the family who offered the food. In the second, the swami graciously accepts the food and then retires to a quiet place to eat alone. Both of these manners are widely accepted and understood. It's up to the saint how he or she wants to accept the alms.

I followed the boy into the other temple. The mother was standing on the temple steps with a bucket of water and she washed my feet. Then her son wiped my feet with a clean cloth and they took me inside. The mother asked me to sit on a wooden platform while she waited on me. She lit incense and doted on me like I was her own son, with so much love and devotion and I was greatly moved.

Then the mother served me sweets and they both fanned me while I ate. This was my first meal as a swami and I felt that God was already taking care of me.

Tears rolled down my face when I left and I knew, then, that I would never, ever, worry about myself. The Lord is always the well-wisher of everyone and it's His goal to bring happiness to everyone. (*From: "From the Heart of the Lotus, the Teaching Stories of Swami Kripalu," by John Mundahl, Monkfish Books, Rhinebeck, NY 2008)*

Bapuji as a wandering swami in western Gujarat, India, circa 1943. Photo from archives of Umesh Eric Baldwin.

March 11th
(This is the Spiritual Pursuit)

To be a seeker is to be of pure character. To find faults in oneself and strive to remove them is the spiritual pursuit. In the absence of faults, virtues come naturally and become rooted in the inner self. So long as the good influence of virtue fails to pervade the mind, there is no advancement in the spiritual pursuit.

Ceremonial bells inside mountain top temple, Nepal Himalaya. Photo by Umesh Eric Baldwin.

March 12th
(Continue on with Your Journey)

It is best to grow slowly, but steadily, on the spiritual path. Our progress is directly proportional to our love for the goal, because only love can create the necessary strength or power to progress. The seeker must acquire many spiritual qualities. If we try to obtain them all at once, we'll fail. One by one, we should try. Getting rid of a bad character trait is just as good as acquiring a new one. When we travel from one place to another, we naturally separate ourselves from the old place as we approach the new place. With great patience and self-forgiveness we should continue on our journey.

Notes to Myself

March 13th
(Only Babies are Born in our Town)

Once a man entered a town and asked a small child: "Have any great men and women been born in your town?" "Oh, no!" The child answered, "Only babies are born in our town." And so it is with faith and devotion. The love for God doesn't happen all of a sudden. It starts small, like a baby, and grows bigger and bigger. It develops best when we have a chance to live with a guru and observe his or her pure character. When this faith and devotion matures, it is a great blessing, because it helps us progress on the spiritual path during difficult times.

weknowyourdreams.com

Notes to Myself

88

March 14th
(Self-Observation without Judgment)

Each night, review your day and learn from it, but treat yourself with love. When workers spread fresh cement on the floor, you cannot walk on it for two or three days. If you walk on it before it's ready, you'll leave footprints forever. And so it is on the spiritual path. We must be patient. Some things take time.

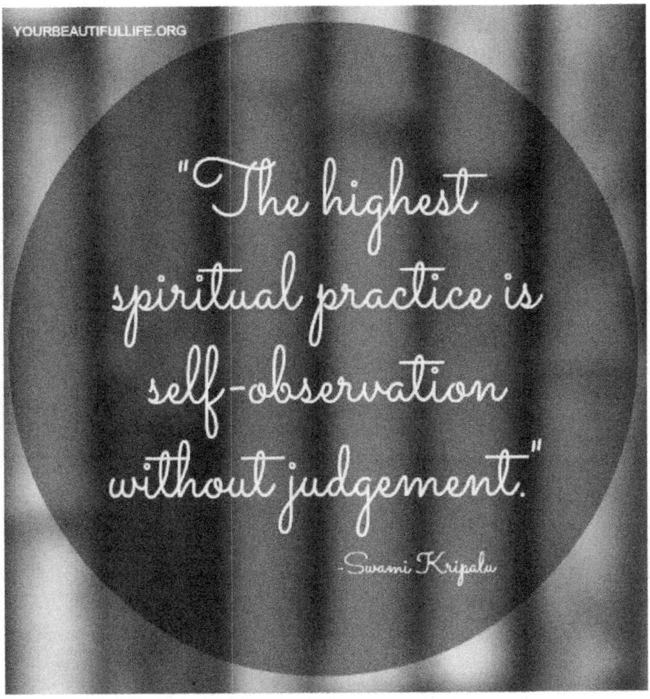

www.ayurvedadynamics.com

March 15th
(Elevate and Purify Your Mind)

Soil gives life to a tree and the tree will continue to live as long as it receives nourishment from the soil. Our soul gives life to our mind and our mind will live elevated and purified only to the extent that it inclines towards our soul. To elevate and purify your mind, contemplate scriptures, repeat japa, pray and keep good company. These practices will eliminate the dreadful shadow of sorrow.

Bapuji at his writing desk in Muktidam. Photo by Pandavi Anna Pool. 1978.

March 16th
(Spiritual Pliers)

A pair of pliers is used to tighten and loosen things and to straighten things out. Wouldn't it be nice if we had a tool to straighten us out? For that we need the tools of self-discipline and right conduct. Right conduct is achieved by right company, and right company is achieved by discrimination, by knowing who and what is good for us and who and what isn't good for us.

Notes to Myself

91

March 17
(Kings without Crowns)

Our growth as individuals, families, societies and nations is directly proportional to our spiritual wisdom. This wisdom, the glory of India, is found in the wisdom of its spiritual masters and saints who were, and still are, the ageless examples of selflessness, purity and spiritual discipline. They are the great possessors and caretakers of this universal wisdom. They are kings without crowns.

Ramana Maharishi

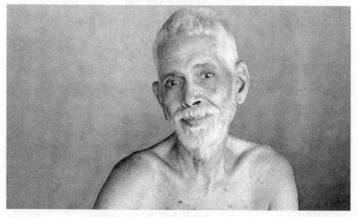

consciouslifenews.com

<u>Notes to Myself</u>

March 18th
(The Light of Self-Knowledge)

Ordinary knowledge comes from some person or object outside of ourselves, but spiritual knowledge comes from our Soul. Lasting peace comes from here, not from the outside world. Traditionally, in India, the Guru is the instrument who makes this connection possible. Just as a lit candle lights an unlit candle, the Guru removes our layers of ignorance so our inner candle can be lit. This is the light of Self-Knowledge. But you must be careful. Take a long time to select your Guru.

www.thepeaceseekers.com

<u>Notes to Myself</u>

93

March 19th
(Selecting a Guru)

When the desire for spiritual growth awakens, we realize the value of a Guru. Like a jeweler who recognizes a valuable diamond, an evolved seeker recognizes a master. We should then not change Gurus very often. Restless seekers take initiation from numerous Gurus and yet attain nothing. The scriptures call such seekers ungrateful and dishonest. Nor should we rush into taking a Guru. Neither should we follow the advice of others. We should first stay in contact with the Guru for a long time. We should observe the Guru's spotless character and feel intense faith and love for this person. Then we should humbly ask for initiation as a disciple.

Photo from "www. natural meditation. net."

94

March 20th
(Is There Money in the Safe?)

When choosing a Guru, don't worship the individual. Worship the character of the individual. If a safe is beautiful, but has no money in it, why should we be interested in it? But if the safe is full of money, and we want the money, we should try to open it. The money in the safe is the character of the Guru, so before you select a Guru, spend time with the person, the more time the better, and see if there is any money in their safe. If there is, then that person is worth your time.

Bapuji with Swami Vinit Muni and Swami Rajarshi Muni in India.
1973. Photo by Umesh Eric Baldwin.

March 21st
(The Yogic Scriptures)

People select saints according to their own temperament. One person likes a scholar, another a renunciate, another an ascetic, another a yogi, another a devotional saint. Those who worship knowledge, consider what is said, rather than who is speaking. Those who worship character, consider who is speaking, rather than what is said. Great acharyas then give lengthy explanations to beginners and terse teachings to advanced students devoted only to yoga practice. The elaborate teachings for beginners are provided in the Vedas, Upanishads, Darshans, Puranas and other true scriptures. The terse teachings for advanced seekers are given in the Brahma Sutras, Yoga Sutras, Narad Bhakti Sutras. and other true scriptures.

Notes to Myself

96

March 22nd
(From One Illusion to Another)

If we compare our life to a boat, then the Guru is the captain and the world is the ocean. The opposite shore is the Lord. Those who are having fun on this side, have no need for a guide, as they are happy where they are. For many years we stay on this side of the ocean. We go from one illusion to another thinking we are happy.

Notes to Myself

March 23rd
(A Great Truth)

The spiritual masters have all taught the same thing:

"Have trust in God."

This is not a lie. This is a great truth. This thought didn't come from an ordinary person. God is! As soon as we have complete faith that God is, all our activities will be taken care of.

Villager in the lowlands near the Nepal-Indian border. Photo by Umesh Eric Baldwin.

March 24th
(This is the Way to Live)

This world is an ocean of pain. It is foolish to try to find happiness in it. The purpose of the world isn't to give us happiness. It's to give us pain, so we will turn to the Lord. Consider all unhappiness and pain as the prasad or grace of God, and give your life to Him. This is the way to live.

Bapuji in India, circa 1970. Photo from archives of Umesh Eric Baldwin.

March 25
(Good Friday)
From, "The Passion of Christ," by Swami Kripalu

The crucifixion had begun in the afternoon, but not a single ray of sun was visible. The entire sky was covered with dark clouds. It was as if the day had turned into night. The whole country was enveloped in darkness. It appeared that all of nature was deep in sorrow. The moment of death approached. The crowd was silent. Absolute silence pervaded the entire scene.

As before, Christ's loved ones could only observe in sorrow the second part of this drama. When a person is in a helpless situation, his body, prana (life force), chitta (mindstuff) and intellect are not able to take even one step toward freedom.

Christ's pain-racked body hung on the cross. Blood streamed from both his hands punctured with nails. The thorny crown created agony each time he moved his head. The stripes on his back made by cruel whips constantly oozed blood. Yet Christ continually prayed to the Lord. Indeed, the appropriate time for prayer is during periods of extreme pain or happiness.

It is normal in such painful situations for the person to be vengeful toward the enemy. But Christ was a saint. Even during his last stages of death, when his consciousness surfaced after bathing in the sacred pool of his prayer to the Lord, there was no animosity in his mind. Christ opened his eyes. His compassionate glance fell first on his loved ones who were sobbing bitterly. His gaze, a nectar of love, showered upon them.

He gazed at them for only a few moments, but the effects of this nectar would last for years to come.

Then Lord Christ's gaze fell on those who scorned him. In that moment he was everyone's benefactor. His mind was completely absorbed in praying to the Lord.

He spoke spontaneously. "Oh, compassionate Father, forgive them. They deserve to be forgiven for they do not know what they are doing."

Only an extraordinarily great master could express kindness toward his enemies. Christ, indeed, was the Son of God, and he did not forget that fact even at the last moment of death. At that moment, he was able to practice what he had preached. This was indisputable confirmation that he was the Son of God.

Then the executioners placed one of his feet on top of the other and began to hammer nails through them. More blood flowed. Christ's head fell to one side. Tears flooded from the eyes of his loved ones. Their hearts seared with pain. Even in such a painful situation, Christ's heart manifested tender prayerful melodies to the Lord.

Evening approached.

Although engrossed in prayer, it was apparent to Christ that death was quickly approaching. Only a few moments remained.

Lord Christ lifted his tear-filled eyes skyward. His body was pathetically pale. His parched lips parted unconsciously. Suddenly he verbalized his silent prayer.

"Oh, my beloved Lord, why have you abandoned me?"

Surely this was intolerable pain, but it was not the pain of death. It was the pain of love. It was the expression of a devotee to the Lord. It was devoid of concern with worldly matters.

His loved ones heard the words of this last prayer and were convinced that Lord Christ was indeed God's devotee. If he had been otherwise, he would not have been able to utter those words in such a difficult situation.

His enemies also heard his words, but they were not touched. They misinterpreted the statement as being Lord Christ's confession of being totally helpless because his God did not help him in the least.

A soldier soaked a sponge in wine mixed with vinegar and offered it to Christ at the tip of a stick. "Here," the soldier said. "Suck a little of this wine to wet your parched throat. This will enable you to speak loudly."

Many in the crowd roared with laughter.

This was vile mockery. Even a heartless person would hesitate to commit such an evil deed. But this was an animal disguised as a man who believed and made others believe he was religious. He had no knowledge of religion. This was not disrespect for a person; it was utter violation of religion. It was a totally evil action.

Another man, in order to intensify the mocking, stopped the soldier. "Brother, it is no use. You won't get any results."

A third person pretended to argue. "Oh, don't give up. Wait. Let's see if Elijah will come to save him. Why are you so impatient?"

Christ was absorbed within. None of the actions of those on the ground below him had attracted his attention. Once again, a pathetic prayer slipped out of his mouth. "My beloved Lord, why have you abandoned me?"

He uttered the words with a groan. His voice became a mere croak in his parched throat. His loved ones were overwhelmed by his words. Those words have become immortal and have spread throughout the world.

Then a soldier pierced Christ's side with a spear. Streams of blood and water gushed out. His entire body was now covered with scarlet blood that ran down and soaked the ground beneath the cross. Finally, Christ's prana became free from bondage to his body and set forth on its pilgrimage to heaven.

The cruel hearts of his enemies were satisfied. The hearts of his loved ones were torn. One of his beloved ones sobbed, "The lamp of Jesus' life has been extinguished."

Another loved one consoled the other by wiping away his tears.

"Why are you talking like this? He wasn't an ordinary oil or ghee lamp that can be extinguished. He was an extraordinary global lamp radiating with divine light. Night is approaching. He has merely set for a while. Tomorrow morning his light will rise again in the East."

(From: "The Swami Kripalu Reader, Selected Works from a Yogic Master," by John Mundahl. CreateSpace. 2014.)

March 26th
(The Supreme Religion for Everyone)

There are five scripturally prescribed spiritual disciplines: Non-violence, Truth, Non-stealing, Brahmacharya and Non-attachment. When any of these are broken, our mind becomes restless. Just as a flame flickers in a windy place, our mind flickers unsteadily without the shelter of these spiritual disciplines. Ahimsa, or Non-violence, is the first of these disciplines. It means *to not cause distress, in thought, word, or deed to any living creature.* Its primary position signifies its primary importance. It is the seed of the other four disciplines. When this seed sprouts, Truth, Non-stealing, Brahmacharya and Non-attachment manifest spontaneously. The practice of non-violence is religion without equal. It is the supreme religion for everyone.

wwwmarkwhitefineart.com

104

March 27th
(Character-building)

Character-building is necessary for life to flourish. It can be built best with the bricks of yama and niyama. One of these practices is straightforwardness, which means simplicity, or purity of the body, the organs and the mind. When we practice purity of the body we're concerned with using our body only for worthy actions. When we practice purity of the sense organs, we're concerned only with sights worth seeing, words worth hearing, and smells worth smelling. When we practice purity of mind, we contemplate only those thoughts that are simple and innocent and determine never to deceive anyone.

www.lashala.es

March 28th
(Leave Flying to the Birds)

My message to you today is this: You are all on the yogic path. Don't get sidetracked by yogic powers. They are useless to a true yogi. The yogi has to give them all up in the end, anyway. The purpose of the spiritual path is to perfect your character, not to amaze others with yogic powers. Why do you want to see a yogi fly? Aren't you busy people? Don't you have better things to do? What purpose would it serve? Leave flying to the birds.

commons.wikimedia.org

March 29th
(Project Kindness)

Many people come to me in India for marriage counseling. I tell them all the same thing: "Stand in front of a mirror and practice speaking kindly. Look at your face and eyes when you do this and project kindness. And don't think this is play-acting. Truly look at your face and see what you are projecting to others." I say this because few people are born non-violent. Milarepa, the great Tibetan yogi, committed murder. When he understood what he had done, he repented and took up the spiritual path, and after intense sadhana he became a great yogi.

Milarepa. *journal.phong.com*

March 30th
(The Spiritual Path and the Worldly Path)

The spiritual path is more difficult than the worldly path. Worldly people just say and do whatever they want, whenever they want, with no regard for anything except getting their own needs met. When we step upon the spiritual path, we make a commitment to stop acting like this. This sets off an internal war. The ego does not want to die. This war is called sadhana and we all have to fight it if we are to experience God-Consciousness.

Notes to Myself

March 31st
(Agreement Sees Virtues)

The major characteristic of unconditional love is non-conflict. When conflict is born, love gradually decreases. Conflict is poison. At first, it creates disease in the body of love. Later, it creates unconsciousness. And finally, love dies altogether. It is blind and cannot see truth. It sees faults, instead, while agreement sees virtues.

Notes to Myself

April

April 1st
(Compassion)

Just as a morsel that drops from an elephant's mouth can feed a thousand ants, a charitable act from a powerful person can alleviate the pain of countless people. Since our world is the Lord Himself, and the Lord is our world, serving an individual is as good as serving the Lord Himself. A one-rupee note, a five-rupee note, a ten-rupee note, a fifty-rupee note, a hundred rupee-note, a thousand-rupee note, are all called notes. But they don't have the same value. Similarly, everyone's compassion is called compassion, but they don't have the same value. The compassion of a mighty person is like a valuable currency note from which a suffering person receives much benefit.

Notes to Myself

110

April 2nd
(Truly the Wise Proclaim)

Truly the wise proclaim that love is the only path, that love is the only God, that love is the only scripture. Impress this thought upon your memory and chant it constantly if you want to realize your dreams of growth. Only love purifies the body and mind. Love is the all-seeing divine eye and the wish-fulfilling touchstone. Every living being is a stream of love. Let us allow someone to taste our love and let us taste someone else's love. Love flowing into the life of another is the source of our happiness, and love flowing into our own life is the source of another's happiness. This is a universal law.

www.twitsnaps.com

Photo from archives of Umesh Eric Baldwin, winter, 1978,
Sumneytown, Pennsylvania.

April 3rd
(Saints Turn a Deaf Ear to Praise)

Saints turn a deaf ear to praise. Praise makes us proud and careless. Bitter censure is the remedy for our faults, while sweet praise destroys our virtues. In the beginning, a devotee's aim is the realization of God. However, when people are attracted to him by his vows, rules, love of God and good conduct he loses his purpose. This mass popularity leads him on the wrong path. Deceit, pride, and false shows of humility increase. By attaining the status of master, he loses forever his status as student. The result is the downfall of the saint.

Photo from archives of Umesh Eric Baldwin. Summer, 1978.

April 4th
(Service Purifies All)

Service is the religious path of right action for all. Love is dharma. The family, being the capital of love, is the head office of service. Service is like a thread that connects the flowers of family, society, nation and universe into one beautiful garland. Without it, unity is not possible. Service is the strength of love that creates heaven in hell and turns strangers into loved ones. Service is the river of love. It purifies all.

Notes to Myself

114

April 5th
(The Little Elf the Tongue)

Lord Krishna says in the Bhagavad Gita that we should speak in a way that harms no one. Yet, most of us cause pain to others by what we say. Our body is heavy and our tongue is light, but it causes great damage. Look how cunning it is. It lives among 32 teeth always safe and protected, and yet it causes us continuous problems. The little elf needs a giant to control it. When the elf is angry, all the ingenuity of the giant is needed to check it.

Notes to Myself

April 6th
(Few People Possess True Knowledge)

The teacher in a normal classroom is an average person. The Guru is an extraordinary one. Teachers are numerous. Gurus are few. A teacher can have a bright mind, but no character, and still find work, but a Guru needs both knowledge and character. The light from the sun removes darkness on earth, but it cannot remove spiritual darkness, the ignorance of our own true nature. The Guru's light can do this, so his or her light is considered greater than even that of the sun. He replaces inner darkness with inner light, the light of knowledge. This knowledge removes attachments to our mind and body and leads us to the lotus feet of the Lord. This is true knowledge and few people possess it. It changes an ordinary person into an extraordinary being.

Bapuji in India.
1974.
Photo by
Umesh Eric
Baldwin

116

April 7th
(People with Great Faith)

People with great faith have great joy in their heart. They are one-pointed. Their faith is the driving force in their life. It keeps them moving in one direction. They can't be distracted, be it faith in God, faith in a new business deal or faith is some creative effort. As long as the flame of their faith remains lit, they progress toward their chosen goal. In this bhajan that I sang for you this morning, the sadguru has given a siddhanta, a spiritual teaching: *Keep the flame of faith always burning in your heart. Never let it be extinguished.* Life will challenge our faith continually, but true devotees keep the flame of their faith lit. Their faith comes from their heart and they know that faith in God, or guru, is a beautiful thing.

tricia-danby
.deviantart
.com

April 8th
(Giving a River its Own Water)

The Guru is the world's most charitable person. The Guru gives the gift of knowledge which removes suffering. What can we possibly give to someone so powerful that he needs nothing? Dedicating anything to him or her is like giving a river its own water or a plant its own flower. The Guru already owns everything we could possible offer. How can we, the poor refugees, offer anything to the place of refuge? Anything we give to the Guru isn't a charitable donation. It's simply a token of affection.

Bapuji in India, 1973. Photo by Umesh Eric Baldwin.

118

April 9th
(The Great Mahatmas of India Need Nothing)

The great Mahatmas of India need nothing. How can we serve such a person, then? The service we give them is only ordinary. The seeker does whatever he can to stay close to the guru…washes a dish …fills a water pot…cooks a meal. But once a piece of cotton touches perfume, it smells like perfume. This is the result of contact. Now tell me, did the cotton serve the perfume or did the perfume serve the cotton?

Bapuji in his ashram in Malav, India, circa 1965. Photo from archives of Umesh Eric Baldwin.

119

April 10th
(How to Obtain Spiritual Knowledge)

If you find a person who arouses good feelings in you, you should regard him as your Guru and serve him. You must keep yourself in eternal contact with his pure soul. In the Bhagavad Gita, Shri Krishna taught his dear disciple, Arjuna, how to obtain spiritual knowledge: "Dear Arjuna, go to a knowledgeable and master Guru, and receive the highest knowledge that will liberate you from suffering, by bowing down, serving him, and asking questions with humility." There is a difference between conditional service and selfless service. The disciple serving selflessly is close to his Guru and receives much greater reward than the one who serves with selfish motives. If a disciple doesn't love his Guru with a pure heart, he cannot progress spiritually. Without love for your Guru, knowledge isn't possible.

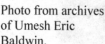

Photo from archives
of Umesh Eric
Baldwin.

120

April 11th
(Yama and Niyamas)

Yama and niyama build a person's character so thoroughly that by sincerely practicing them one ceases to be an animal, grows into a real human being, and can even transform into the Lord. Although their practice is arduous, fear of failure is unwarranted, because we are only required to practice yama and niyama to the best of our capacity.

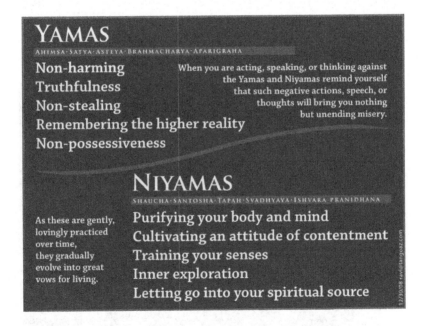

YAMAS
AHIMSA·SATYA·ASTEYA·BRAHMACHARYA·APARIGRAHA

Non-harming
Truthfulness
Non-stealing
Remembering the higher reality
Non-possessiveness

When you are acting, speaking, or thinking against the Yamas and Niyamas remind yourself that such negative actions, speech, or thoughts will bring you nothing but unending misery.

NIYAMAS
SHAUCHA·SANTOSHA·TAPAH·SVADHYAYA·ISHVARA PRANIDHANA

As these are gently, lovingly practiced over time, they gradually evolve into great vows for living.

Purifying your body and mind
Cultivating an attitude of contentment
Training your senses
Inner exploration
Letting go into your spiritual source

12/30/08 ravi@tangoaz.com

www.tangoaz.com

121

April 12th
(We Cannot Progress Spiritually if we Harm Others)

Ahimsa, or Non-Violence, is the first yama and it is regarded as the most important. We simply cannot progress spiritually if we harm others. However, because we are human, we are all violent. It is only a question of degree. Hurting someone physically is the most obvious. Yet, when we use harsh words towards someone, it is also violence. The scriptures tell us to speak sweetly and without selfishness. Since most of our interaction is with our family, this is where violence in any form, especially speech, is likely to occur and also where we can practice Ahimsa daily in our speech and actions.

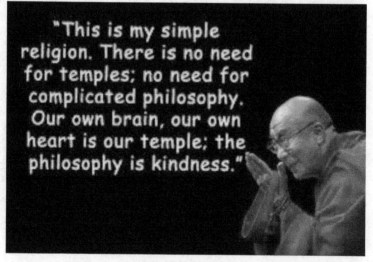

"This is my simple religion. There is no need for temples; no need for complicated philosophy. Our own brain, our own heart is our temple; the philosophy is kindness."

www.pinterest.com

April 13th
(Isn't This Idol Worship?)

Anger is a powerful distraction to the mind. We must overcome it if we're to arrive at lasting peace. It may visit us from our external surroundings or at any moment from within our own minds. When these thoughts arise, there's no switch to shut them off, but one trick is to start a new train of thought that doesn't disturb us so much. Devotees in India use pictures and statues for this. Westerns may think that this is idol worship, but it isn't. The pictures and statues create such a loving response from the devotee, that the devotee's mind is washed in love and becomes one-pointed and ready to pray and meditate.

Parvati, symbolizing strength and wisdom, holding the sword (Khadga) to destroy all ignorance. North India.

Photo by Umesh Eric Baldwn.

123

April 14th
(A Home for All)

Can a lifeless building like an ashram provide divine protection? An ashram is alive, not dead. An ashram, set in the world, has the same significance as a statue set in a temple. It is a divine symbol of the Sadguru and the home of tapas (spiritual disciplines). It the guru's home, God's home, and the home for all. Only God's home can be a harbor of peace, a place of happiness and an abode of bliss.

A porter
in the North
India Himalaya.
Photo by
Umesh Eric
Baldwin.

April 15th
(My Blessings are All I Can Give You)

Today, I was extremely touched by your pranams. I wanted to cry. The way you came up to me on your knees each holding a flower was overwhelming. My blessings are all I can give you and I give you those from the depths of my heart.

Bapuji's hand. Photo from archives of Umesh Eric Baldwin.

April 16th
(The Vow of Brahamacharya)

The vow of brahmacharya is the highest vow and also the most difficult. It is most powerful when practiced at a young age. It greatly purifies the body and mind of a young person and makes them very strong. Yet, this vow shouldn't be forced on anyone. It should be accepted by our own free will. It is easier to dance on the edge of a sword than to practice this vow. You must remain constantly awake and stay in control of yourself and understand perfectly how to practice this vow before you begin. That's the key.

The grand Himalaya, the abode of Lord Shiva. Photo by Umesh
Eric Baldwin

April 17th
(An Experiment)

All my life I've deeply contemplated the subject of celibacy or brahmacharya. Truly, this is the most important subject for the entire world. I have contemplated this subject for only 50 years, whereas the ancient sages of India contemplated it for thousands of years. Our current understanding of celibacy is different from the ancient concept of brahmacharya, and is superficial by comparison. Their knowledge transcends the limits of body, mind, and intellect and has entered the unapproachable realm of the soul. Repression of sexual energy leads to perversion. Sublimation of sexual energy through yogic disciplines leads to immense spiritual power. Just as energy generated by steam or electricity can power machines which perform great tasks, the celibate yogi can also accomplish amazing tasks by conserving sexual energy. To produce steam, water and fire are necessary. To produce spiritual power, pranayama and celibacy are necessary. Experiment with pranayama and celibacy under proper guidance for a year and a quarter and see for yourself.

Notes to Myself

April 18th
(Don't Let Difficulties Stop You)

Difficulties will come. When you sit still and do nothing, they're merely sleeping. When you get up and decide to act, they wake up, too, and get in your way. Learn to face them properly. They bring out your inner strength. That is their purpose. Don't stop with difficulties. Continue on and have faith in God.

<u>Notes to Myself</u>

128

April 19th
(This is the Work of the Soul)

The family is the proving ground. Make a firm commitment to create a heavenly home environment. When we are living with others in a close environment, there will be differences of opinions and ways of doing things. So every day we can practice tolerance, patience, forgiveness and gentleness. You will fail many times. You won't become an expert all at once. It takes practice and patience, but this is truly the work of the soul.

joequatronejr.com

April 20th
(Peace in the Family)

The first requisite in life is that peace reign in our household. To establish peace in our household we will have to win the hearts of every individual, big or small. When peace is established by force it isn't peace, but a regime of terror. Divinity is born out of the peace founded on love. Peace and tolerance are born when we learn to control our mind and emotions. We should try to deal with every family member with love. If we seldom consider the feelings of others and only concern ourselves with our own state of mind, disagreements, friction, and dissatisfaction are born. If we are agreeable with others, they become agreeable with us. Instill the love of God into your family. Without surrender and service, love cannot evolve.

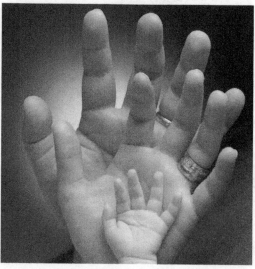

jesusplus.org

April 21st
(Fault-finding)

Don't look upon the faults of others. By doing so, your own consciousness will become impure. If you hold something dirty and stinking in your hand, what happens? Your hand will stink, too. When you dwell on the faults of others, you dirty your mind. If you must dwell on faults, dwell on your own faults. And if someone points out your faults, try to bear it and change.

Photo from
archives
of Umesh Eric
Baldwin. 1978.

April 22nd
(The Straw on the River Ganges)

Man, who lives in darkness, thinks: "Look at me! Look at all the things I'm doing!" Yet, God is so great that He hides behind His creation. We should give thanks to Him and remember Him from whom we draw our strength.

One day the river Ganges was flowing beautifully out of the high Himalayas. The sun was bright on the pure, clean water. There was a sudden gust of wind and the wind picked up a straw and dropped it on the current of the river.

"Look at me!" The straw said. "This river is so beautiful! I'm passing flowers and woods and I can see all the mountains and overhead the sky is blue!"

The river kept flowing and passed one holy place after another.

"Look at me!" The straw said. "I'm passing all the holy places of India."

They came to a place where a lady was gathering water by the side of the river. She had a bucket and she dipped her bucket into the river and the straw went into her bucket.

"Look at me!" The straw said. "This lady will carry me throughout the town. I've found the holy place meant for me."

"Good by, straw," the river Ganges said. "I'm going to keep going, but you stay here if you want. I've taken you to all the holy places and I'm pleased that you found a place that you like. But first, though, don't you think you should thank me?"

"Thank you?" The straw said. "For what?"

132

"For carrying you," the river said. "You floated in my current and I brought you here."

"No!" the straw said. "Didn't you see me swimming? I wasn't floating; I was swimming."

"Little straw," the river laughed. "You were floating, not swimming. You did nothing on your own. You didn't have the strength to swim on your own in my water and if you had, you would have swam all over the place and not arrived at this holy spot. Go now if you want to, live here and be happy, but give thanks to God."

And the river left. *(From: "From the Heart of the Lotus, the Teaching Stories of Swami Kripalu," Monkfish Books, Rhinebeck, New York 2008.)*

www.happytellus.com

The Ganges in Haridwar, India.

133

April 23rd
(The Medicine of Chanting)

If you're worried, if you're suffering, take the medicine of chanting. This is indeed the real medicine. If I tell you that mantra is the best doctor, I would only be telling you part of the truth. Mantra is the entire hospital. Just as we clean our body by taking a bath, we clean our mind by chanting the Lord's name. Once you bathe in that way, your mind becomes pure and clean.

Notes to Myself

April 24th
(Your North Star)

Sometimes our dramas are clearly a drama to us and don't fool us or disturb our minds. At other times, our dramas appear real and disturb us very much. In those moments, keep silent and remember your mantra. Just as the North Star indicates the direction of true north, your mantra continually points toward your goal, Peace.

www.skywatch.com

April 25th
(This World is an Ocean of Pain)

Everything we perceive is the Lord's maya. It is our great fortune just to be able to say a few prayers to Him. This world is an ocean of pain. It's sheer foolishness to try to find happiness in it. The Lord alone is the ocean of bliss. We must worship Him and accept any pain we encounter as His grace. Hold tightly to your mantra and believe with your whole heart that you are clinging to the holy feet of the Lord.

Notes to Myself

April 26th
(A Wonderful Thing)

Singing, dancing, clapping and mantra chanting are a beautiful way to meditate because you're engaging all of your senses. That's an easier way to meditate than just sitting and watching your mind. Sitting quietly in meditation is difficult because you will be flooded with thoughts and tempted to react to them. Clapping, singing and dancing make all the thoughts run away. What a wonderful thing!

Bapuji in India, circa 1960. Photo from archives of Umesh Eric Baldwin.

April 27th
(A Radio Full of Static)

Lord Krishna says in the Bhagavad Gita, to control the mind and to control the wind is the same. Extraordinary seekers understand this and before they enter their meditation room, they attend to their thoughts first. Are they angry at someone? Are they hurt by something? Do they need to take care of something? The music of the Lord cannot be heard on a radio full of static.

bhavanajagat.com

Krishna controlling the wild fluctuations of the mind in the Bhagavad Gita.

138

April 28th
(Even Great Saints Become Fools at the Dinner table)

Moderation in diet, Mitahar, is one of the foundations of spiritual progress. It means to eat the precise amount of food required to keep the body alert and efficient. This isn't easy. Even great saints become fools at the dinner table. Try not to eat when you're not hungry. Chew well. Stay conscious when you sit down to eat. Protect your body and your health. Each meal tests our power of discrimination.

Notes to Myself

April 29th
(Divine Knowledge)

Both suffering and happiness are necessary for personal growth. Happiness comes at the end of suffering and suffering comes at the end of happiness. No one suffers either pain or enjoys happiness forever. Liberation means the total eradication of suffering. It is attained only through discriminate knowledge. Only a rare yogi receives such perfect knowledge, but every human being invariably is blessed with a divine ray of knowledge at some point in their life. This knowledge doesn't come from books, but from a genuine experience and it doesn't lose its effects for as long as we live.

Notes to Myself

140

April 30th
(Anahat Nad)

When a highly developed yogi meditates, the yogic fire induces various types of sound to flow from his mouth. This process is called *anahat nad*, or spontaneous sound. All the divine mantras are manifested through *anahat nad*. The first syllable, usually OM, is the seed syllable. The mantra's energy resides here. When a mantra is repeated with strong conviction, or bhavana, it strengthens our will power and purifies our mind through concentration. When a divine mantra bears fruit, the fruit is unshakable faith.

Bapuji doing spontaneous mudras in India, circa 1973. Photo from archives of Umesh Eric Baldwin.

141

May

May 1st
(A Universal Law)

To consume wealth decreases it. To donate wealth increases it. Consumption starts with pleasure and ends with pain. Donation starts with pleasure and ends with pleasure. This is a universal law.

We are what we think. All that we are arises with our thought. With our thoughts, we make our world.

~~Buddha

s266photobucket.com

142

May 2nd
(I Am a Pilgrim of Love)

The path of love is ancient. When I was born, I received the initiation of love. Now, with the same love, I initiate everyone else. Countless times, I have dipped into the world's highest scriptures and received only love from them. Love is my only path. I am, in fact, a pilgrim on the path of love. Lord Love is everything to me. In love, there are no barriers of language, no costumes, no egos, no distinctions of any kind. Only the beloved exists.

Notes to Myself

Photo from archives of Umesh Eric Baldwin. Winter, 1978

May 3rd
The Silent Fragrance of Saints

The unique feature of saintliness is that whoever has this quality is completely unaware that he is a saint. Just as flowers silently exude their fragrance and a lamp silently gives light, flowers in the form of saints silently spread the fragrance of self-restraint and character. Miracles manifested through them are always genuine miracles. Through such miracles we become aware of the reality of divine energy. Just as electricity amazes everyone as it works through an inert object, the energy working through a saint is also amazing. Material scientists have accomplished clairvoyance by inventing the television and clairaudience by inventing the radio. Unaided by these devices, however, great saints use powers generated from yogic disciplines. They can see distant objects by the power of clairvoyance and can hear distant sounds by the power of clairaudience. The material scientist directs his efforts toward the non-soul, away from his Atman. The spiritual scientist directs his efforts towards his Atman. One is a child-yogi. The other is a mature yogi.

May 4th
(Service without Love)

In service without love, a feeling of master and servant exists. There is duality, superiority and inferiority. But in service with love only a feeling of oneness exists. The soul is the master and the body merely performs the action.

Photo from archives of Umesh Eric Baldwin. 1979.

May 5th
(The Names of the Lord)

One of the names for the Lord in Sanskrit means, The Immortal One, or The Indestructible One. These names come from *nad* or spontaneous sound. The scriptures say the names represent the Alpha and the Omega. Whatever name you choose for the Lord, you should feel a heart connection with that name. You should be able to sing it or say it lovingly. The more you say it, the more blissful you should feel. God is bliss, so repeating the name takes you closer to God.

Notes to Myself

May 6th
(Satvic Meditation)

The only purpose for meditation is to have a satvic meditation, that is, a calm, peaceful meditation. If your mind is disturbed, don't sit for meditation because you will only dwell on your disturbing thoughts. We should quiet our minds first. This happen best in solitude.

Bapuji's meditation room in Muktidam in the United States. He did sadhana here from 1977-1981. Photo by John Mundahl, 2007.

May 7th
(The Meditation of the Yogi)

When we are angry, we are meditating. We're holding on to one thought line in a powerful way. We're absorbed by it, engrossed in it. All other thoughts are forgotten. Similarly, when we're absorbed in sexual thoughts, we're also meditating. But the meditation of the yogi is satvic, that means 'pure.' It doesn't cause excitement or disturbance in the mind or imbalance in the body. It increases self-control. We should meditate on the higher things to obtain peace, bliss, and happiness.

Notes to Myself

May 8th
(The Power of Satsanga)

Satsang means to sit in the company of truth. In satsang, we purify our minds and increase our devotion through contact with a saint or other truth seekers. At that time, we should relax our mind and give up worldly thoughts. We've accumulated countless wrong thoughts and desires from many incarnations and satsanga will gradually eliminate these thoughts. Only that which can change the direction of our mind can affect us. Satsanga has the power to do that.

A natural forming Shiva Linga, Garhwal Himalaya, North India.

Photo by Umesh Eric Baldwin.

May 9th
(This is known as Surrender)

A ctions performed by the mind using free will are actions performed by the individual. They are binding. They create karma. Actions performed through the promptings of prana, free from the desires of the mind, are called action-less actions. They are not binding. This is known as surrender.

Bapuji doing spontaneous mudras, 1979. Photo from archives of Umesh Eric Baldwin.

May 10th
(Tapas)

Through the fire of self-discipline, the body and mind become purified. This is called tapas. Tapas means to heat. It is the fire of self-discipline. Tapas of the body keeps the body clean and healthy. Tapas of the mind creates peace, gentleness, silence and self-control.

What are spiritual disciplines?

Intentional practices that deepen
our experience of God's grace
by creating space for God's Spirit
to do his transforming work in us.

May 11th
(The Entire World is One Family)

Noble saints in India, after taking the vow of renunciation, travel everywhere in society and keep the same affectionate, selfless relationship with the world as a whole as they did with their original family. Sanatan Dharma, the eternal religion of India, prescribes that saints continually develop the feeling that 'The entire world is one family.' Thus, the renunciate cultivates a more expansive feeling of love for his world-family to which he subordinates his feelings of love for his original family.

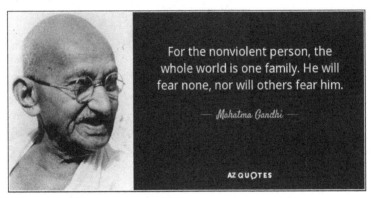

For the nonviolent person, the whole world is one family. He will fear none, nor will others fear him.

— Mahatma Gandhi —

AZ QUOTES

www.azquotes.com

Notes to Myself

153

May 12th
(This is the Spiritual Pursuit)

To be a seeker is to be of pure character. To find faults in oneself and strive to remove them is the spiritual pursuit. In the absence of faults, virtues come naturally and become rooted in the inner self. So long as the good influence of virtue fails to pervade the mind, there is no advancement in the spiritual pursuit.

Notes to Myself

May 13th
(Mother's Day)

Today is Mother's Day, a very auspicious day for the mother. The mother is the first and only true guru. She is the one who bestows happiness and bliss on her children. The mother is the banyan tree of the world under which everyone can take refuge and receive solace and peace. In the entire world, there is no other tree bigger than the mother, the banyan tree, and there is no other refuge like the mother's tree. "Mommy," as little ones call her, is not just made of skin and bones. Mommy is the sweet of all sweets. She is the nectar. When we get old and sick and are taking our last breath about to make our final pilgrimage, we may not remember God, but we will remember Mommy. "Mommy," we will whisper. "Mommy, Mommy," because Mommy is the only medicine we will want at that time. She is the only medicine for all of our diseases and unhappiness. She bestows countless gifts upon her children, yet never thinks of herself or expects anything back, not even gratitude. How can we pray to her? How can we honor her? There is no way. We cannot possibly repay her service. We can only bow down to her with tearful eyes and utter, "Oh, Mommy." This is the word she loves to hear best. This is my prayer on this holy day, that all of my children receive blessings from their Divine Mother and from their own mothers, as well.

May 14th
(Prayer)

I've been doing yoga sadhana for 27 years and have come close to death 5 times, very close, and yet by the grace of God I have survived. It is prayer that has sustained me. It is truly a miraculous tool.

Summer, 1978. Photo from archives of Umesh Eric Baldwin.

May 15th
(The Lord's Play)

The Lord's play, or maya, is totally beyond our grasp. I'm surprised that I, accustomed to living within the four walls of my residence in India, have suddenly come to America. The strong force of your love has brought me here. My only purpose in coming is to meet my grandchildren. I haven't come to spread yoga or religion. To me, in fact, this whole visit seems like a dream, or the Lord's maya

Photo from archives of Umesh Eric Baldwin. Winter, 1978.

May 16th
(Take Care My Words do not Escape You)

Follow a regular schedule and fulfill your daily obligations with purity of mind. Thus, every action is followed by a change in the heart. Each action will seem dear to you. You must know that you have gone one step forward in sadhana when there is no dislike in you for anyone and you are always in a pleasant mood. The change occurs first as a decrease of egoism and then is replaced by humility. Take care my words do not escape from the cage of your mind! You may forget me, but do not forget my words. Do not neglect, but try to follow my advice enthusiastically as far as possible. Be loving, good, enthusiastic and pure.

Notes to myself

Photo from archives of Umesh Eric Baldwin. Summer, 1977.

159

May 17th
(Tolerance)

When we practice tolerance, we definitely feel pain, but this pain is short-lived compared to the bliss and contentment that tolerance generates. Tolerance is fruit-bearing genuine religion itself. This religion should be practiced everywhere, not locked up churches, temples and ashrams. We should take it with us wherever we go. A temperament which tolerates others is a genuine step toward true religion.

Notes to Myself

May 18th
(Who Can Serve the Guru?)

After much thought, I decided that it's impossible to be of any service to the guru. The only person who can serve is someone who has the capacity to serve. The healthy can serve the sick. The rich can serve the poor. The learned can serve the ignorant. How can we serve the guru, then, who needs nothing? We can't, of course. We serve the guru so that we can be close to the guru, so that we may receive His grace and blessings. By staying close to the guru, we become familiar with his thoughts and actions and soon begin to know his soul, his essence, too. The guru is full of peace and joy and the disciple feels this bliss.

Notes to Myself

May 19th
(Sanatan Dharma)

A long time ago, India had a high civilization. The driving force behind this civilization was Sanatan Dharma, the eternal religion. We could call it *deva dharma*, the religion of the Gods.

Sanatan Dharma has four pillars: scripture, temples, yogis and society. The scriptures are the soul of the religion. The temples are the body. The yogis are the prana, or life, and society is the heart.

Each pillar can give birth to the other three. That is, from the scriptures, alone, you can read about Sanatan Dharma and establish the religion. From the temples, alone, you can establish the religion because all the secrets of yoga are written in the language of samadhi on the temple walls and in the statues. From the yogis, alone, in their sadhanas, Sanatan Dharma is re-born over and over. And from society, alone, all the principles of Sanatan Dharma are preserved if people sincerely want to practice them.

Notes to Myself

May 20th
(How I Met My Gurudev)

On this beautiful morning you have reminded me of my beloved Gurudev. I thank you for that. Beloved Gurudev is my whole life. I'm alive on this earth only by His grace. My life would be meaningless without His love. I can't describe in words to you the nature of my Gurudev, who He was, what He was about. An artist may paint a picture of the sun, but no matter how good the picture is, that sun can't give light. No matter how I describe my Gurudev to you, you can only know Him through your imagination, which will never be the true picture of Him.

I was young, only 19 years old. I was extremely ambitious, but unable to attain what I really wanted, so I was disillusioned with life. From childhood I had been attracted to the feet of the Lord. The Lord was my solace, my support, and my life. I didn't know anything about sadhana at that time, so I used to worship God according to the tradition of my family.

After the death of my father, our family was thrown into poverty. I couldn't bear this pain, even though I was only 7 years old, so I made a firm vow that I would give my whole life to God and bring happiness to my suffering family.

I had to drop out of school even though I was a bright, motivated student. I loved to read, but our family needed money and I tried to do what I could.

When I was 19, I left for Bombay to try to find work, but my heart was full of darkness. Finally, I decided it was better to commit suicide and go home to the Lord. I planned the whole thing; I was going to throw myself under a train.

Our family worshipped the Lord in the form of the Divine Mother, so I went into a nearby temple to

163

worship the Divine Mother for the last time before I killed myself.

It was about 9:00 o'clock at night. I entered the temple in total despair and my heart melted and tears rolled down my cheeks. I went to the altar and bowed down and burst into even more tears. I had come simply to say good-by. I was going to kill myself at midnight. The statue of the Divine Mother didn't look like stone to me; she looked alive. Her eyes were full of love and I was there to ask permission for what I was about to do.

The caretaker of the temple knew me and he tried to console me, but he couldn't. I just kept crying. And at that auspicious moment, my Gurudev entered the temple. I was thirsty for knowledge. I had been to many different saints. I had read books about mantra and tantra and magic and had visited all the saints, but I had never trusted any of them. For me a guru had to be someone I could give my whole life to, *nothing less*, so I had given up trying to find a guru. I had totally stopped thinking about it.

Gurudev entered the temple and he said just one word,

"Son."

I can't describe to you the sweetness of that word, no matter how hard I try. He lovingly placed his hand on my head and then he hugged me.

"Come with me," he said.

He was a total stranger and yet His love was so profound that I immediately yielded to Him. We walked outside the temple and then he sat down on the steps of one of the shops.

164

"My son," he said. "Are you going to commit suicide? Suicide isn't good."

"Oh, no!" I said. "No! No! No! I would never do that!"

I wasn't a dishonest person or a liar. I was just in shock that someone knew my deepest thoughts.

"You're a sadhak," he said. "And you must speak the truth. Tonight you were going to throw yourself under a train." And then he described my whole scheme.

When he was finished, I bowed down to him and touched his feet.

"Please forgive this child," I said.

"Come and see me next Thursday," he said, and he gave me an address.

Thursday is the day of the guru in India and I discovered that he always gave darshan on that day. But I arrived late. I tried hard to be on time, but I failed to do so. I bought a garland of flowers for five rupees with great love. I had little money and you could buy a nice garland for one rupee, but I selected a beautiful garland for five rupees with great love.

I placed the garland around his neck and then gave him a dandwood pranam, lying down completely flat on my stomach. He looked at me and the nectar of love flowed from his pure, beautiful eyes.

"My son, swami, you have come," he said, stroking my head.

The word, swami, surprised me.

"I'm not a swami," I said.

"My son, I've called you swami because you're going to be a swami in the future."

165

"Me?" I gasped. "Oh, no! I don't think so! I can't do all that begging!"

"It's true that swamis beg for food," he said. "But they aren't beggars as you understand it. They're beggars of love. You're going to give your love to the world and you're going to receive love from the world."

I was crying now and even though I was crying, I was happy.

Gurudev had known that I would be late that day and he had instructed the gatekeeper to keep the gate open for me, even though he normally ended darshan promptly.

"One child will come," he had told them, "and he will be late, but let him in."

Then he had saved a spot next to him for me to sit, while all the other disciples had to sit at a distance. But there was great joy on their faces.

"I've come here for one young disciple who will come to us today," he had told them. "I'll initiate him into swamihood and then I'll leave. He'll become a great yogi."

Gurudev attracted me to his feet when I was 19. I stayed with him for a year and a quarter. It's by his grace that I've been able to maintain this sadhana for so many years. There's only one thing that I want to do with my life, and that's to do sadhana for as far as it will take me. I have no attraction left for money, fame, or name. My only desire is to remember the name of God.

(From: "From the Heart of the Lotus, the Teaching Stories of Swami Kripalu," by John Mundahl. Monkfish Books, Rhinebeck, New York 2008)

May 21st
(The Divine Sounds of Yoga)

Many years ago when I was sitting in meditation, I chanted this same Ram dhun that I chanted for you this morning. The tune emerged automatically from within. I didn't try to chant it or arrange the words or the tune. It just came spontaneously from within. This is called *anahat nad,* or spontaneous sound. This happens in yoga sadhana when the prana and apana both begin to rise up. When they join together and work in the visuddha chakra, or throat chakra, sound is produced. The yogi spontaneously chants Om, Ram, and the immortal mantras such as the Gayatri and Om Namo Bhagavate Vasudevaya, your mantra. These are divine sounds to the yogi and so the yogi says these sounds are from God. When we use sound willfully to create music we can enchant our mind and make it one pointed. It's useful then as a tool for meditation."

www.pinterest. com

167

May 22nd
(Ram Chanting)

We just finished chanting a Ram dhun. Ram is truly one of the great wonders of the world. In India, it is a name for God. All of the greatmasters throughout the glorious spiritual history of India recommended Ram chanting. They all decided the same thing, independent of each other, that Ram is the best name for God. Ram is for everyone, Indian and non-Indian. It knows no nationality. This is because when prana intensifies through shaktipat and rises up into the throat chakra, the mouth opens and Ram chanting begins. This is an important milestone in yoga. It means the seeker has found the right direction. So everyone in India chants Ram and Ram is coming here now because India has found America.

Garhwal
Himalaya,
North India.
Photo by
Umesh Eric
Baldwin.

May 23rd
(The Eternal Path Back to God)

P rayer is the first step of yoga. It is the silent speech of love. It is the light of love. It is the only eternal path back to God.

www.foldedinprayer.com

Today my prayer is…

169

May 24th
(The Spiritual Journey is a Journey Within)

We don't have to walk a single step to embark on our spiritual journey. The spiritual journey is a silent journey. It is the journey within. We *do* need fast-moving vehicles, however. These vehicles are the yamas and niyamas, the spiritual disciplines of yoga. We prepare for our journey and travel safely by observing these disciplines and practices.

vimeo.com

Notes to Myself

May 25th
(Sadhana Takes Patience)

We can undertake and complete several vocations in our life. However, the attainment of God is so difficult that even if one puts all his effort and concentration into the task, he may not succeed in a lifetime. The seeker who wishes to attain God should close the gates to all activities and keep open only the gate to the Lord. To attempt to attain the Lord Almighty means to sacrifice one's whole life to this holy cause. To make a garland, we bind together flowers on a string. The seeker must sacrifice his soul, tie all his actions on the thread of God, and be hit by Cupid's arrow in his love for God, or he can't be an upashak and make real progress. Sadhana takes great patience. When I first started my deeper sadhana, I thought I would be finished in six months.

Notes to Myself

May 26th
(When we Love Another)

Great souls love everyone in the world, but we must start by loving those people we can. When a husband puts his eyes in front of his wife like two cannons, love seeks the first open door and escapes. It's the same for a wife, if she acts that way. Love is a form of God. When we love another, God is born in our heart. There is another word...attachment. It looks like love, but it isn't love. Once love awakens, it can never be destroyed. Attachment comes and goes. It's there in the morning, but disappears in the evening.

www.pinterest.com

May 27
(The Great Masters Chose Silence)

The great masters realized long ago that purification of speech was extremely difficult, so they chose silence. They just gave up trying and chose not to speak. Most of us can't do this, so the other option is to speak just a little and try to remain conscious when we do. This spiritual practice is called *mitdarshan* in Sanskrit and it means *to speak only when absolutely necessary.* We know that the headstand is a difficult posture, yet purification of speech is more difficult than a thousand headstands. First, try to keep silent for two hours a day. Then gradually increase it to one whole day. Pick a day, say Thursday, when you will practice doing this and try to remain alone. This will create heat or *tapas.* You do this intentionally. You observe your thought pattern while remaining silent.

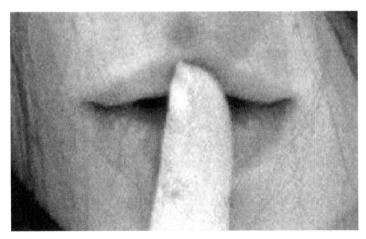

icrowdnewswire.com

173

May 28th
(Unsurpassed Remedies for Diseases)

Fasting and abstaining from sex are unsurpassed remedies for diseases. Through fasting the diseases are insulted and leave the body, while good health enters uncalled. When much waste matter collects in the body, we become sick and lose our appetite. This is natural and is an involuntary fast. When we voluntarily fast, the appetite increases and thus voluntary fasting is difficult. But when Mother Nature inspires an involuntary fast, we are saved and not eating is easy.

Nature set the correct example through our loss of appetite, but we are often such fools that we force a person who is naturally fasting to eat and he is made worse. We mistakenly advise that the fasting has made him weak and that one can't live without eating, not realizing that gluttony was the cause of his disease and loss of appetite in the first place. One can observe that often people are weak regardless of how much they eat, while others are strong in spite of not eating.

By overeating, we overburden the digestive system and much of the food goes undigested. This undigested food gets pushed forward, becomes purified and causes diseases like coughing, acidity, flatulence, impure feces, urine, perspiration and bad breath. After considering everything, it is wiser to limit the amount of food you eat and remain healthy, than to overeat and become a victim of disease.

174

May 29th
(Asanas)

Asanas are useful to men, women, children, the old, the diseased and the healthy. One should do asanas on an empty stomach, at least four hours after a meal, morning and evening. After finishing asanas, one should wait one hour before eating.

Asanas should be done under the strict guidance of an expert. Whether one is sick or healthy, one should do pranayam (breath control exercises) for at least one month before beginning with easy asanas. After one's strength and knowledge have increased, one should progress to more difficult asanas.

Before trying a new asana, one should study the picture of the asana carefully, read the description thoroughly and then, without haste, arrange the limbs in the pose of the asana. Bodily progress is maximum when the asana is done with full understanding. When done without understanding, asanas can harm the physique.

One should accompany an asana with its complementary asana in order to maintain balance and thus exercise the whole body. According to one's preference, strength and understanding, one should choose asanas for the head, neck, chest, abdomen, spine and limbs.

One should not become over-eager and strain the body while doing asanas. Also, as soon as the body starts to tire, one should stop doing asanas. Asanas that are the most beneficial should be done only within set limits of time and strength. One cannot do difficult asanas in the beginning and one should not torture one's limbs to achieve them.

Bapuji doing spontaneous postures early in his sadhana, circa 1950. Photo from archives of Umesh Eric Baldwin.

May 30th
(Concentration)

Concentration is the perfection of the art of action. An artist uses concentration to perfect her art, whether it is drawing, music, dancing, elocution, writing, or any other. Since concentration is an important aspect of yogic knowledge, the activity of the artist is essentially yogic and the artist is a sadhak. The sense faculties of a painter, musician, dancer, orator or an author are active while drawing, singing, composing, dancing, lecturing or creating a masterpiece of literature. Thus, concentration and the senses are intensely related.

Through concentrating our senses, either good or bad results may result. We should ignore concentration of the senses that leads to degradation, and practice only concentration that elevates our life. By sublimation of the senses, not only are the sense organs calmed, but the mind also becomes soothed. So this sublimation is considered superior to the concentration of the artist or scientist, though their concentration can be considered permanent if they ignore temptation when it crosses their path. The art that comes with such concentration makes a deep impression on society.

177

May 31st
(Suffering Fills the Holes in our Colander)

As long as we are attracted to the world, as long as we like the sensual delights, spiritual knowledge can be put in our lap and we will walk away from it or not recognize it. But when we decide that we've had enough, when we begin to walk away from the attractions of the world by our own willpower, by conscious choice, then we begin to receive spiritual knowledge. We begin to recognize and value its importance. As long as our mind is the victim of the temptations of the world, we won't experience the in-depth failure, the suffering and pain needed to drive us unto the spiritual path. If you dip a colander into the river, you won't come up with any water. The mind of a worldly man can't hold spiritual knowledge because it's like a colander. Arjuna, in the opening of the Bhagavad Gita, is at this point. His suffering is deep. He sees no way out and it's at this point that we turn to God. Suffering fills the holes in our colander and we become capable of holding the spiritual water, the knowledge.

The suffering of Arjuna in the Gita.

June

June 1st
(Love is Not Far Away)

Lovers have been quarreling since ancient times. Some attest to the sweetness of love. Others attest to the pain. Those who understand the true nature of love, however, dissolve their disputes easily. The truth is there is neither joy nor pain in love. Love is simply sweet. The joy and pain of love are our own illusions. Love is simply blissful compassion. It is not far away. It is as close to us as our heart. We can find it living there without walking a single step in search for it.

photodoto.com

June 2nd
(The Dharma of Service)

The dharma of service is the dharma of love, the very embodiment of love. In whomever love arises, divine vision also arises, so that service does not remain inaccessible to him. The person who becomes the embodiment of love does not remain an ordinary human being. His faults are transformed into strengths and he becomes an extraordinary person.

www.pravsworld.com

Notes to Myself

180

June 3rd
(Repeating the Name of the Lord in a Group)

When you repeat the name of the Lord in a group, the benefits are unique. If 250 people repeat the name of the Lord just once, it's like one person repeating the name of the Lord 250 times, because your ear hears 250 voices. So, chant the Lord's name both in groups and by yourself. This is the best way to occupy your idle mind. It gives rise to love and where there is love, there is God.

www.aviaryforyou.com

<u>Notes to Myself</u>

181

June 4th
(In Ancient India)

In ancient India many kings were initiated into religious life at age 51, when they retired. They walked into the forest lived in a simple dwelling and pursued the sadhana of liberation. Numerous Brahma Rishis enlightened with the Supreme Spirit also inhabited the forests. They were personifications of Brahma and were lights of knowledge, yoga, devotion, dedication, and nonattachment. Although these sages had powerful emperors as disciples, they observed the vow of renunciation and asceticism and wore only a loincloth. True asceticism differs from willful sacrifice. Asceticism is a state wherein desire for worldly pleasures, whether they are available or not, doesn't arise at all. Asceticism is a synonym for renunciation. As our love for God increases, attraction for worldly pleasures is destroyed. Asceticism means the actual dislike of worldly pleasures and extreme liking for God

Notes to Myself

June 5th
(Love, the Highest Mantra)

Love is God, Himself. It is the highest mantra. Love your family as yourself. Consider their happiness your greatest happiness. Give others so much love they can't be without you. They should feel your absence. Their hearts should leap when they see you, such is the depth of your love. To nourish this kind of love, you must continually burn like a lamp and for that you have to practice self-sacrifice.

Photo from archives of Umesh Eric Baldwin. Summr, 1980.

183

June 6th
(The Purpose of Prayer)

The cause of all unhappiness is separation from God. The cause of happiness is reunion with God. The nature and purpose of prayer, or remembrance, is reunion with God.

thesundaymass.org

My prayer today is…

184

June 7th
(Chanting is Like Taking a Bath)

Just as we clean our body by taking a bath, we can clean our mind by chanting the Lord's name. This is like taking a bath, too. Once you bathe in that way, your mind becomes pure and clean.

Bapuji in India meditating as young man, circa 1944. Photo from archives of Umesh Eric Baldwin.

June 8th
(The Fire of Tapas)

Tapas means to heat. Tapas is the fire. Fire purifies metal. The fire of tapas is the fire of self-discipline. That's what heats the body and mind. Through the fire of self-discipline, both the body and mind become purified.

TAPAS

"Glow/Heat"

Austerity, penance, an ingredient of all yogic approaches with the goal of transformation and self-transcendence.

www.yogajournal.com

Notes to Myself

June 9th
(Purifying the Mind)

A purified mind works in harmony with prana. Prana is one-pointed, dedicated and devoted to the well-being of the entire person. Mind by its very nature is duel, divided and hence deceiving. Prana is whole and works for the whole. Mind is fragmented, distracted and distorted. The purpose of Pravritti Dharma is to purify the mind. This is the foundation for Nivritti Dharma.

Photo from archives of Umesh Eric Baldwin. 1978.

June 10th
(Like a Stone in a River)

I have lived here for two years now, but I have lived like a stone in a river. I haven't learned your language. I haven't seen much of your beautiful country. I'm as blank as when I first arrived. Yet, I've always loved languages, learning and reading very, very much. When I was a child, my bedroom was a special place because I filled it with books. At night, I read until late at night. I read even at suppertime while eating. My mother would get angry. We had kerosene lamps back then and my mother would blow out the light and say, "Now go to sleep!" I would almost cry because I wanted to keep reading so badly. Finally, she just took away the lamp. Now I don't read so much, but I reflect deeply on what I read. I may read one sentence or one sloka and dwell on it for a long time. It's a form of meditation for me. And when I give written advice, I ask myself: Am I practicing that? Am I able to do that? And if the answer is, no, then I don't write it. How can I ask someone to do something that I myself can't do?

www.pureflorist.com

June 11th
(The Love in your Eyes)

Whatever I have said about the language of love and our relationship of love is due to my seeing the love in your eyes and feeling the tide of sentiment in your hearts.

Summer, 1977. Photo from archives of Umesh Eric Baldwin

189

June 12th
(Sahaj Yoga)

In sahaj yoga, vajroli mudra is included in the ten important mudras in ancient yogic scriptures. In the sexual act, the apana is thrown outside the body with force. In yoga, the apana is forcibly drawn into the body. This internal suction is known as vajroli mudra or yonimudra.

The sadhak who practices Sahaj Yoga achieves vajroli mudra and also khechari mudra in a natural way. It happens spontaneously in sadhana due to yogic fire. At first apana vayu is indomitable. Prana is defeated again and again and cannot perform vajroli mudra, the contraction of the genitals, successfully. In the first three stages of samprajnata yoga, apana vayu pushes the semen towards the genital outlet. Prana performs vajroli mudra and attracts the sexual fluid in the opposite direction. In the fourth stage of samprajnata yoga, the prana becomes very strong and the apana becomes weak and vajroli mudra is performed successfully.

During the practice of the first three stages of samprajnata yoga, beautiful images of women and men appear to the meditating yogi and tempt the sadhak. But when the sadhak enters the fourth stage of samprajnata yoga, rajoguna and tamoguna become weak and satvaguna becomes dominant. Sensuality or lust no longer trouble the sadhak. Just as children remain unmoved by passion when they see each other naked, the yogi in the final stage of samprajnata yoga isn't moved to passion by the appearance of naked women.

190

After the achievement of vajroli mudra, the sexual fluid of the sadhak is not destroyed, so he or she can become an urdhvareta and achieve a divine body, divine consciousness and complete detachment.

Photo from archives of Umesh Eric Baldwin.

June 13th
(Crying at the Feet of the Lord)

Crying openly at the feet of the Lord is the best prayer. Nothing else can compare to such a prayer. Poetry is beautiful, full of decorative words, but do these words touch the heart? When children cry, do they cry in the form of a poem? Do they cry using decorative language? No, and yet their cries touch the mother's heart.

The mountains of the Himalya, the abode of Lord Shiva. Photo by Umesh Eric Baldwin.

192

June 14th
(Father's Day)

Today is Father's Day in your country. It will be an unforgettable day in my life. I was extremely touched by the way you came up to me and offered me your pranams on your knees. There was great humbleness in that. Your love was coming from the very depth of your being. Really, if you were six or seven years old, I would have picked you all up and placed you on my lap, just to hold you. If you can love everyone with the same love that you loved me today, your life will be full of happiness. The scripture of love is ancient. We cannot start love at 7 in the morning or 8 in the evening. We must hold it in our hearts all day long.

Father's Day, June, 1977. Photo from archives of Umesh Eric Baldwin.

193

June 15th
(A Father's Day Blessing)

If we don't leave the attraction for worldly things, how can the love of the compassionate Lord be born in our hearts? When our heart is filled only with love for the Lord, then our progress back to His home will be quick. Our progress on the spiritual path is directly proportional to the love in our heart. On this Father's Day, I pray to the Lord that He, the Father of us all, may come into our hearts. As children, we may forget Him, but He doesn't forget us. He will always care for us. He will always be our support. I give you my blessings today as your spiritual father and grandfather. May the love of the Lord be born in us all.

Notes to Myself

Photo from archives of Umesh Eric Baldwin. Winter, 1979.

195

June 16th
(Wherever There Is Love, There Is God)

Wherever there is love, there is God. Happiness, peace and joy live there. Today you have converted this chapel into a temple of love. The scriptures of Sanatan Dharma say that the three most important people in our lives are our mother, father and guru. Through them love comes into our lives. They are the personification of love, dedication and service. This is their divinity. To serve them is a divine pleasure. This past half hour has been extremely blissful for me. The love that you offered to me as your spiritual grandfather has filled my heart. As each of you came up to me on your knees, the light of your love went deep into me. A stream of love poured from your heart into mine. Our hearts merged, just as a river merges with the ocean. I felt like I was swept away, that I was drowning in your love. I will never forget it. Nourish this love. Keep it going. Don't allow it to go out. Give it to everyone.

www. timespages .com

196

June 17th
(Sanatan Dharma)

India is the land of the *rishi-munis*. These high souls lived in sacred places in the forests and mountains and did their sadhanas determined to find answers to our deepest questions. This went on in India for thousands of years. To my knowledge, no other culture has taken the search for truth to this extent.

They wrote down their final truths in the scriptures of Sanatan Dharma and left nothing to speculation. Everything had to be proven. Even though these scriptures are old, they remain precious, because these are the realized truths of these great souls.

Sanatan Dharma was born in the woods. Nobody propagated it or felt the need to propagate it. Just as the sun doesn't come down from the sky to spread its light, so too, Sanatan Dharma spreads its light wherever it's found. It doesn't wander into villages, towns or countries looking for converts.

Its guiding principle is *Vasudeva Kutumbakam, the entire world is one family.* Wherever it goes, it creates love and harmony. This is true religion. True religion acts like a needle and creates oneness out of duality. Non-religion, or adharma, acts like a scissors and cuts oneness into pieces.

197

Photo from archives of Umesh Eric Baldwin. Summer, 1977

June 18th
(Prayer is the First Step on the Path to God)

Prayer is the first step on our path to God, the path of yoga. Just as the earth nourishes the trees and allows them to grow, prayer allows us to grow and evolve as spiritual beings. It is the silent speech of love. It is the light of love. It is the eternal path that leads us from untruth to truth, from darkness to light, from death to immortality. It is the only immortal religion.

www.svdpmpls.org

Today my prayer is…

June 19th
(Two Types of Spiritual Teachers)

The word in Sanskrit for highest truth or realized truth is *siddhante*. One who has realized the complete truth, the final truth, is a Siddha. Such a master teaches realized truth. This knowledge is called *siddhante*. There are two types of acharyas, or spiritual teachers. One type gives spiritual knowledge from books. They are thinkers. The other type is the yogi. The yogi gives spiritual knowledge that he has experienced or realized. Thought that has been realized is siddha thought. It's proven thought. It's thought that has truth behind it. Thought that hasn't been personally realized, that has been learned from books, is simply movement of the mind. It's weak. The great masters, the siddhantes, gave only realized truth.

Photo from:
"www.natural
meditation.net"

June 20th
(The Boy Who Soiled His Pants

Once when I was a young swami, I was visiting the town of Sisogra. There was a 14 year old boy there who liked to be at my side. That particular year there was a poor mango crop, so the people of the town used to ration their mangoes and bring some to me. I used to give some of the mangoes to this boy. I stayed for about 14 or 15 days. Then I left for a neighboring town about 5 miles away.

"Bapuji," this boy said as I was leaving, "I would like to come with you so that I can keep eating mangoes."

"That's fine," I said. "You can come."

The neighboring town wasn't far away and we arrived there shortly. The people there had arranged for me to lead spiritual discussions and I told the organizers,

"Please, if you can, give mango juice to this boy twice a day, in the morning and in the evening. He loves mangoes."

"Yes, Bapuji," they said. "We'll do that."

They gave the young boy a room in the ashram where I was staying and he received mango juice twice a day, morning and evening. He was happy.

One day, the ashram workers were cleaning all the bathrooms and all the water pots that are used in bathrooms in India. Suddenly this boy called to me.

"Bapuji!" He called. "I have to go to the bathroom real bad! I can't hold it any longer! What should I do?"

201

"Here!" I said quickly. "Take this big water pot with you and go outside. There's a bathroom there."

"No!" He said, "That pot's too big! I'll spill all the water!"

"Then just run outside quickly and I'll follow with the pot," I said.

My room was on top of a hill near the temple of Madhu and you had to go down a few steps to get outside. Mango juice is purgative and the boy lost control going down the steps and soiled his pants. He turned to me full of rage.

"Why did you tell these people to bring me so much mango juice? They force me to drink it twice a day!"

"No," I said softly. "It's you who doesn't know how to drink the juice."

This same thing will happen in yoga sadhana. Everything must be done with proper understanding and great patience.

(From: "From the Heart of the Lotus, the Teaching Stories of Swami Kripalu," by John Mundahl. Monkfish Books, Rhinebeck, New York 2008)

June 21st
(Dwelling on the Faults of Others)

Don't dwell upon the faults of others. If you do, your own consciousness will become impure. What happens when we focus on the faults of others? Simple logic will give us the answer. What happens when we hold something stinking in our hand, or put something stinking up to our nose, or put something stinking into our mouth, or put something stinking into our pocket and carry it around for days? We stink, too. We can't dwell on the faults of others without dirtying our own mind. This is a *siddhante*.

Bapuji's altar in Muktidam where he did sadhana in the United States from 1977-1981. Photo by John Mundahl, 2007.

June 22nd
(The Nature of the Saints)

A seeker should firmly decide: *I will look only at my own character, not at the faults of others.* This is the nature of all great saints. If we must dwell on faults, then we should dwell on our own. This is acceptable on the spiritual path, but not the other. And even here, we should be careful. We should examine our own faults free of judgment, not with guilt or regret, as this, too, disturbs our mind. Self-observation without judgment is the way to grow. It is highly prized on the spiritual path.

Bapuji, just before his death, still meditating 10 hours a day pursing the Divine Body. Before the Divine Body can manifest, the physical body must become completely emaciated. Photo from archives of Umesh Eric Baldwin.

June 23rd
(Life without Mercy)

Life without mercy is worthless. When parents love their children, we may call it mercy or grace or love. This love should be in our eyes and in our hearts and we should express this love to others in our speech and actions. This is mercy. We all need it, because we are all suffering. The best mercy is when we feel the pain of others. This is compassion. Compassion is generated when we truly hurt for another person. We aren't merely helping them to be nice. We're helping them because we hurt in our heart for them. Their pain has touched us.

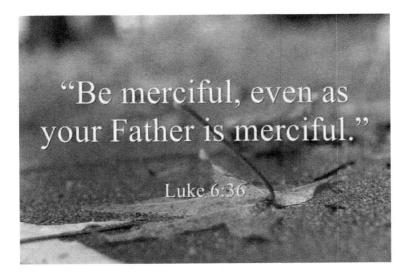

"Be merciful, even as your Father is merciful."

Luke 6:36

biblicallypure.com

June 24th
(Surrender to Prana)

In the Bhagavad Gita, the concept of surrender is presented in a deeper way. The Gita is a book for total liberation and here surrender means *surrender to prana in sadhana.* The seeker must be able to completely relax the mind and let prana do whatever it wants to do during meditation.

The deeper meaning is that our life should be guided by prana, prompted by prana, not our mind, which is subject to duality and the pain that comes with it. In kundalini sadhana, the seeker sits for meditation, ignites his prana, and then drops his mind and watches prana do all the actions. This is called *Sahaj Yoga,* natural yoga, or spontaneous yoga, and there is no karma from these actions because they come from God, prana, and not our mind, which is the instrument of ego. This is called *inaction in action* because there is no karma from these actions.

Eventually, the yogi's mind becomes so purified by this sadhana that even when the yogi is mixing with the world again, his actions still come from prana because his mind is purified and it isn't a hindrance. Prana, God, is flowing cleanly through the yogi's mind and all external actions.

When I speak of prana, however, I'm not talking about the prana that is in the air. That is prana, too. I'm talking about the prana that erupts and intensifies in sadhana. That prana is much finer than the prana in the air. It's the Lord, the Prana of Pranas.

206

Can you imagine how subtle and fine that energy is? We can't see the prana in the air because even *that* prana is too fine, and yet this higher prana is even finer than that. If you can't see the child, how can you possibly see the Father, the Prana of Pranas?

To see the Prana of Pranas and great divine beings like Krishna and Jesus, we need a divine eye. This is the eye of knowledge. It can only be seen in meditation. When one enters samadhi, the divine eye opens and you see everything through this divine eye. You see the truth, then, *that everything is one, everything is connected and everything is God. This is part of the Brahmavidya, a Sanskrit word meaning the divine knowledge.*

Notes to Myself

207

June 25th
(Faith)

The word for faith in Sanskrit is *shraddha*. This word is subtle and quite deep because it implies the strength of the individual, or the character and personality of the individual. In other words, whatever a person has faith in tells a lot about that person. Some people have faith in science, others in business, others in their own effort and others in God. People with great faith have great joy in their heart. They are one-pointed. Their faith is the driving force in their life. It keeps them moving in one direction. They can't be distracted, be it faith in God, faith in a new business deal or faith is some creative effort. As long as the flame of their faith remains lit, they progress toward their chosen goal. In this bhajan that I wrote and sang for you, the sadguru has given a *siddhanta*, a spiritual teaching: *Keep the flame of faith always burning in your heart. Never let it be extinguished.*

Notes to Myself

June 26th
(Faith Must Come from Your Heart)

Faith must come from your heart. It shouldn't be on the surface. To have faith in a guru is really the greatest of fortunes. We can't see God, but we can see a guru, and to *really* trust this person, to *really* love this person and know that this person would never hurt us, gives birth to devotion, the highest means of progressing on the spiritual path. Naturally, this doesn't happen all of a sudden. It develops slowly. A seed is small when it's planted and gradually becomes a large tree. A tree just doesn't suddenly appear.

<u>Notes to Myself</u>

June 27th
(Faith)

Once we have given ourselves to God, that is committed ourselves to the spiritual path, we shouldn't ask for it back. It's not good to give something and then ask for it back. Once we have truly offered our life to our spiritual growth, we should accept whatever comes, be it happiness or unhappiness, and see it as truly in our best interest. This is faith, or *Shraddha*, in Sanskrit. Our faith should never be shaken. We have no need to be afraid of anything. We should simply rest at the feet of the Lord and be happy.

Durga riding the tiger near a Shiva temple, North Indian Himalaya.
Photo by Umesh Eric Baldwin.

June 28th
(The Purpose of Yoga Sadhana)

Yoga sadhana exposes all our faults. That is the purpose of sadhana. The sadhak (the yoga practitioner) bows at the feet of the Lord each day and offers his faults to God in sadhana, and the merciful Lord accepts them because He doesn't want us to suffer. Sometimes only God can remove our faults. We're too weak on our own. Then we should pray to Him for help.

Bapuji slept on a simple mat in Muktidam where he did sadhana in the United States from 1977-1981. Photo by John Mundahl, 2007.

June 29th
(There is Power in a Name)

There is tremendous power in the name of the Lord when we call upon Him. You may ask, how can there be power in a name? Isn't there power in the name of a rich man or a famous athlete? Don't we use their names to sell products? Think, then, how much more powerful is the name of God. We can use this power to sooth our troubled minds. God accepts our anger and calms our passions.

Notes to Myself

June 30th
(Prayer)

If we do nothing with our life except sincerely pray, our life will be worthwhile.

Lord, keep me
in the spirit
of prayer.

www.agodman.com

My prayer today is…

213

July

July 1st
(The Power Source behind our Movements)

Usually, we feel like we are the one doing things, that we are the doer, but spiritual seekers feel like there is a power source behind their movements. To them, there are two power sources: the power of the Lord and the power of the individual, or the ego. When we sit in a car or airplane, we feel like we're moving and we are, of course, but we aren't doing it. The car or the airplane is moving and we're simply along for the ride. When the desire of the individual fuses with the desire of the Lord, the work becomes Divine work. When the desire of the individual separates from the desire of the Lord, it causes difficulties. So the cause of our problems is our ego will, our individual will.

Notes to Myself

July 2nd
(Contact with a Saint)

One who finds a high saint has truly received the grace and blessings of the Lord. This contact brings peace of mind and knowledge of sadhana. How can we practice sadhana without knowledge? Just as we need money to start a business, we need knowledge to start sadhana. By the grace of the guru, or saint, we attain a higher consciousness, and by the grace of the Lord we attain a guru. Both are connected and when we reach the Lord, our life is fulfilled. Our journey ends.

Photo from archives of Umesh Eric Baldwin. Winter, 1978.

215

July 3rd
(A Story of Forgiveness)

Once I gave a talk in a small town. The people loved the talk so much that they wouldn't let me leave, and I ended up staying and giving spiritual discourses there for two months.

A few weeks after I left, a man visited the town and he heard everyone talking about me. He didn't like swamis very much. He had had one or two bad experiences. But he was impressed after hearing the people talk about me, so he told a friend,

"The next time this saint comes, let me know. I would like to meet him and serve him."

About a year passed, and then I was able to visit the town again. The friend sent a letter to this man telling him of my planned visit. The man was pleased and made plans to come and see me.

It so happened that I was late. A kind conductor offered me a seat on a train and I accepted it. At the first stop everyone in our car got off except myself and one other man. He must have been lonely, because as we continued on, he moved closer and closer to me, until he was finally sitting next to me.

"Where are you from?" He asked, and I told him.

"Where are you going?" He asked, and I told him. And then he got mad.

"You're a swami, aren't you!" He said. "And you don't work, do you! You just roam around and around!"

"Yes," I said. "That's what I do."

216

"Why are you wasting your life like this?" He said. "Find a good saint and go and stay with him and serve him. Study, and make something of yourself. I'm on my way to meet a high saint who everyone loves. Come with me and maybe he will help you."

I didn't say anything.

The train reached the small town where I was going and I got off. The man got off, too. It was evening and I needed to cross a river to get to the town so I walked quickly. The man did, too. We came to the river and I gave the boat keeper my ticket.

"Oh, look!" The man said sarcastically. "He has a ticket! He's not traveling free!"

We both got on the small boat, and three or four people immediately bowed down to me. The man laughed and made fun of them. Indian people bow down to any swami and he was laughing at that. Then he noticed that there was a large crowd on the other side of the river and he got quiet. He must have thought that the Mahatma was there already and he was giving darshan.

The boat came to the opposite shore and the whole town had gathered to meet me. Someone had told them in advance of my arrival, even though I was late. When everyone saw me they immediately started chanting and singing and 5 or 6 people rushed to carry me from the boat to the shore so my feet wouldn't touch the muddy water.

"No! No!" I begged, but it didn't make any difference. They picked me up and gently placed me on the shore and then everyone bowed down and touched my feet and offered me flowers.

The man was totally shocked. He just stood there. This was the same man who had been coming to see me. He, too, was late that day and we had met by chance. Then his friend called to him.

"Gopal!" His friend called. "You received my letter! And you've already had a chance to meet swami! How wonderful!"

The man burst into tears. He was ashamed of himself now. He touched my feet and said,

"Only you could bear such harsh words from me. I insulted you very much. Please forgive me."

I embraced the man and held him with love and he was happy.

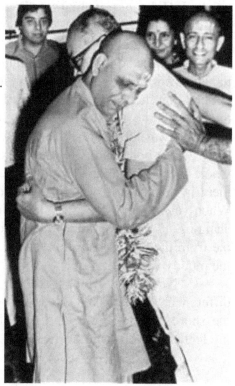

Bapuji in India.
Photo from archives
of Umesh Eric Baldwin.

(Story from, "From the Heart of the Lotus, the Teaching Stories of Swami Kripalu," by John Mundahl, Monkfish Books, Rhinebeck, N Y 2008)

July 4th

(The Religion of Life)

The water of a river flows between two banks and thus is protected. Similarly, if our life flows between the two banks of yamas and niyamas, it is also protected. These banks are religion, itself. The yamas and niyamas are the foundation of all the great religions of the world. The masters consider them to be universal codes of behavior. A religion that doesn't incorporate these disciplines can't prosper long. These commandments are truly the universal religion, the global religion. They are the religion of life. They are the life force of the spiritual seeker committed to living an active life surrounded by others in society. When we sincerely practice the yamas and niyamas we know the art of living. These principles generate skillfulness in action and through such actions we attain truth and purity. These disciplines are the heart of Sanatan Dharma, the path of eternal truth, the eternal religion.

www. gokamayoga. com

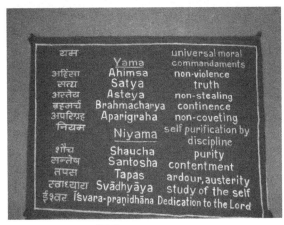

July 5th
(The Spiritual Life Has Two Wings)

The spiritual life has two wings: self-discipline and proper conduct. The door isn't easy, but it's the door to sainthood. This door removes darkness from our consciousness and lights the pure divine light within us. When this light of knowledge is lit, truth is born within us.

Notes to Myself

July 6th
(The Immortal Mantras of India)

The immortal mantras of mankind were first received in India. They came from the sadhanas of great masters, from their immense effort at God-Realization. Other religions have created mantras, but those mantras were created from the mind, not from prana during high sadhana. Man isn't the creator of the mantras in India. The Lord, Himself, created these mantras. This is their uniqueness. They are considered holy.

Bapuji's darshan room in Muktidam in Sumneytown, Pennsylvania. He gave darshan here from 1977-1981 while he was in the United States. Photo by John Mundahl, 2007.

July 7th
(There are Two Types of Wars)

There are two types of wars. One is the war between people. The other is the war within ourselves. When we step upon the spiritual path, this inner war begins. At that time, the lower forces rise up to defeat us and we must fight them. The best way to prepare for this battle is to firmly practice the yamas and niyamas. Maharishi Vyasa, the supreme disciple of Lord Krishna and the author of the Bhagavad Gita, said that success in sadhana is directly proportional to our success in practicing the yamas and niyamas. They are the foundation for our spiritual growth.

Another view of Bapuji's darshan room. Photo by John Mundahl, 2007.

July 8th
(Why Should You Explore Ashram Life?)

Y ou have all come to live in this ashram. Why should you explore ashram life? Plants need watering and special care when they are just beginning to grow. As they get bigger and stronger, they only need watering occasionally. Finally, when they are fully-grown, they seldom need care. We, too, are like that. Just as plants need water, fresh air, nutrients and sunlight to grow, so also we need new light, new inspiration, new karma, new practices and proper surroundings to grow. We can live with others in society, but ashram life provides the unique opportunity to live with a group of people all focused on the same thing: *trying to understand and practice spiritual principles every day, all day.* That is the entire focus of ashram life, *every day, all day*, not just one day a week, or for a few moments when we aren't too tired from working. People in an ashram are all going in the same direction. This support is invaluable in your spiritual quest.

Notes to Myself

July 9th
(This is My Blessing)

Love ties us all together. Our body may have a name, but our soul doesn't. Love ties us together, not names. Let us stay together in love and grow together towards God. This is my blessing. Your loving Dada. (Bapuji chants *Hari Ram*.)

Photo from archives of Umesh Eric Baldwin, summer, 1977.

224

July 10th
(Herein Lies Peace, the Seeker's Goal)

The mind stuff of worldly people is restless due to countless desires. These fickle desires flow in separate directions and keep the person unfocused and disturbed. The individual then becomes extroverted through the five senses. The five senses then come in contact with touch, sight, sound, taste and smells, which create more desires and restlessness. In this way, peace is shattered. However, if we have only one desire, our entire mind stuff flows in just one direction, greatly increasing our strength of character and our ability to attain that desire. The more desires we have, the weaker our character and the greater our unhappiness. For this reason, spiritual seekers attempt to free themselves from *vasanas,* from material and sensual desires. Herein lies peace, the seeker's goal.

Notes to Myself

July 11th
(When We Step Upon the Spiritual Path)

The spiritual path is much more difficult than the worldly path where people just say and do whatever they want, whenever they want, with no regard for anything except getting their own needs met. When we step upon the spiritual path, we are making a commitment to stop acting like this and thus the internal war begins for us.

Summer, 1980. Photo from archives of Umesh Eric Baldwin.

226

July 12th

(How Can We, Who are Human, Attain Divine Love?)

In the beginning, we offer worldly love to our family members. In the end, we offer divine love to God. How can we, who are human, attain divine love? This is done through purification of body and mind, through spiritual disciplines called sadhana. God is divine. When love for God is born in the heart of the devotee, that love is divine. The obstacle to this love is attachment or ownership. A mother shows her child a toy and asks,

"Child, whose toy is this?"

"It's mine," the child says.

"Will you give it to me?"

"No, the toy is mine," the child says.

In this way, children gradually learn to distinguish their own possessions. When selfishness is dissolved for a loved one, however, surrender is born. Surrender is *Prabhu Prasad*, the Grace of God, and it purifies our mind of desires.

www.aamft.org

227

July 13th
(This is the Work of the Soul)

The family is the proving ground. Make a firm commitment to create a heavenly home environment. Practice the yamas and niyamas in your home. When we are living with others in a close environment, there will constantly be differences of opinions and ways of doing things, so every day we can practice ahimsa and the other beautiful yamas and niyamas. You will fail many times. You won't become an expert all at once. It takes practice and patience, *but this is truly the work of the soul.*

www.cutestpaw.com

228

July 14^{th)}
(How to Have a Good Day)

First of all, every day when you wake up, try to think of God first. Do your spiritual practices and then go about your day. When your day is finished and you're tired and tempted to say, "Oh, I shouldn't have gotten mad at so and so," or, "If I had only done that differently today," go to your meditation room again and give your entire day to God and practice your sadhana again. Fill your meditation room with pious thoughts so your mind automatically begins to cleanse itself when you simply enter the room. When you are finished with your evening sadhana, say your favorite prayers and then think about your day a bit. Don't think about the behavior and shortcomings of others. Analyze only your own behavior. When you feel ready to treat those around you with love, leave your meditation room.

Notes to Myself

July 15
(Guru Purnima)

Today, on this Guru Purnima, we are all thinking of the Lord and his saints and the room is full of pure thoughts. We invited the great masters to be with us, from the past and the present, and they are here showering us with their love. May today be a blessing to you all. May today be a memorable day in your life.

In India, circa 1971. Photo from archives of Umesh Eric Baldwin.

July 16th
(Step Firmly upon the Spiritual Path)

Love exists side by side with ahimsa. They are sisters. Love is the opposite of violence. Violence can't enter our life when our heart is full of love. Love even affects the plants, birds and animals that are close to us. This afternoon when Amrit, Vinit Muni and I were coming in the car to see you, one of the ashram cats crossed the road in front of us. A dead mouse was dangling in its mouth. If that same cat would visit us now, it would purr and jump up into our lap full of love and want to be petted; yet it had just committed an act of violence. We are all like that cat. Our behavior is mixed with love and violence. We are capable of both actions. Step firmly upon the spiritual path and grow in love. If that cat was with us now, the love here would render the cat soft and gentle. Our love for those around us can accomplish the same thing.

Ahimsa

✳ kindness and non-violence towards all living things

✳ respect for living beings as a unity

✳ belief that all living things are connected

ahimsainaction.com

231

July 17th
(The Only Journey)

B efore we embark on a journey, we should make proper preparations. There's no journey as important to our lives as our spiritual journey. Ultimately, in fact, our spiritual journey is the only journey. This alone makes life pleasant. Those who haven't taken the first step suffer more than those committed to living a moral life. We don't have to walk a single step to embark on our spiritual journey. The spiritual journey is a journey within. We *do* need fast-moving vehicles, however. These vehicles are the yamas and niyamas, the spiritual disciplines of yoga. We prepare for our journey and travel safely by observing these disciplines and practices.

www.pinterest.com

232

July 18th
(Compassion)

Daya, or Compassion, means *empathy, grace, mercy, kindness or well-wishing.* We are all suffering. There isn't a single person in the world who isn't in some sort of pain. We live in an ocean of pain. It's everywhere. The scriptures of India, in fact, say that the name of the world is the abode of pain. Those suffering deserve compassion and since we are all suffering, we all deserve mercy and kindness. And yet even in this pathetic condition, the compassionate Lord has given us a unique ability, a unique strength: we all can offer compassion to each other, even though we ourselves are suffering.

blog.peacerevolution.net

233

July 19th
(Two Types of Compassion)

There are two types of compassion: purposeless and purposeful. The compassion of the Lord and the great masters is the first type. It is called *grace, a blessing, a favor or boon, or empathy.* In a sense, this is genuine compassion, because the Lord needs nothing back from us, not even to feel good about doing good. It's simply grace. The fortunate soul who has attained the grace of God and guru never needs to seek compassion from others again. God and guru are such infinitely generous donors that they totally transform the recipient of their grace. The seeker's search ends. If God and guru give their grace for no reason, if it's purposeless, why doesn't everyone receive its benefits, then? God and guru shower their grace on every single person unconditionally, but everyone uses it according to their own desires. The seeker doesn't use it for material gain or pleasure. He or she uses it to attain yoga, or union with the Lord. The person is then transformed from one needing compassion into an ocean of compassion for others.

Notes to Myself

July 20th
(The Pain of Others Doesn't Touch Everyone)

The compassion expressed by most of us is purposeful. We show compassion intentionally. It's a form of love. When we see someone suffering, our heart melts. The empathy that arises in our mind and motivates us to extend help is compassion. The pain of someone else becomes our pain and the flame of love, service and dedication is kindled. This feeling of family or close involvement with others, is a divine quality. The pain of others doesn't touch everyone. People who are touched by the pain of others have certain inherent traits in their character. The Lord especially loves these people because God can use them to comfort His suffering children.

Love and compassion are necessities, not luxuries. Without them humanity cannot survive.
~Dalai Lama

July 21st
(This Memory Will Stay With Me Forever)

This past hour we spent together was so sweet and joyous. Today you loved me from the depths of your heart. I am deeply touched. This memory will always stay with me, protected in my heart. You only have to receive love from one person, from me, but I have to receive love from so many. I wanted to cry. I couldn't hold it. If I could pick you all up and hold you in my arms, I would. The way you came up to me, on your knees, each with a flower, the love in your eyes. It was overwhelming.

Notes to Myself

www.pinterest.com

Photo from archives of Umesh Eric Baldwin. Summer, 1977.

237

July 22nd
(Make Your House an Abode of Love)

The highest principle of Sanatan Dharma is *the entire world is one family*. If we are unable to love others, it doesn't matter what religion we're following. It isn't religion. True religion unites us all. Be patient and kind with each other. Make your house an abode of love. Love each other the way you loved me today. There is nothing more that I could ever tell you than that.

www.pinterest.com

July 23rd
(Religion isn't in Books or Temples)

I'm telling you these personal stories because I can't ask you to be loving if I haven't attempted it myself. Religion isn't in books or temples. It lives within us. The first lesson is patience, that is, self-sacrifice, when we're willing, at least for a moment, to put the needs of others ahead of our own.

Sherpa lady on the trail in central Nepal. Photo by Umesh Eric Baldwin.

July 24th
(Our Connection to the Guru)

L ove of God, love of guru, is available to everyone equally. Yet, some disciples receive an extra grace. There's a reason for this. When we produce electricity and connect to it, we receive light. But if the connection is loose, the light goes dim or maybe even out for a while. It's the same thing with love for a guru. If the connection is strong, the light is strong.

thirdmill.org

Notes to Myself

July 25th
(The Key to Spiritual Growth)

Learn self-observation, self-analysis. This is the key, the secret. Before you fall asleep at night, review your day. Go through all of your actions. Note things you're proud of and things you would rather forget. But you must remain objective. You can't judge yourself. To whatever degree you can remain objective, to that degree you will grow, you will receive the light. Through this practice, you can master your mind, intellect and ego and grow closer to God.

Photo from archives of Umesh Eric Baldwin.

July 26th
(Sahaj Yoga)

In Sahaj Yoga when the *Swadhisthana* chakra (second chakra, sex center) is illumined by yogic fire in sadhana, the sexual instinct becomes intense. The sadhak has to sublimate this intense sexual feeling. In order to do that, he or she shouldn't seek the opposite sex.

If it had been possible to sublimate one's sexual feelings with the help of the opposite sex, then this whole world would have been the ideal place for penance and all householders would have become Urdhvareta saints.

During meditation in Sahaj Yoga, control over the genitals is achieved by the practice of siddhasana and mudras that make apana move upwards. In sexual intercourse, neither siddhasana nor the important mudras manifest. As a result, there is no control over apana and thus only pleasure is gained and not liberation.

As the genital region becomes sensitive during meditation, the sadhak's mind becomes full of licentious thoughts. This inevitable situation must be tolerated patiently.

"Arjuna!" Lord Krishna says about this stage of meditation. "Even though one strives to practice yoga and is ever so discerning, his senses lead his mind away by force." (Bhagavad-Gita, chapter 2, verse 60)

The sadhak watches as a witness the various actions performed by prana during meditation. In the same way, he should also watch the sensuous wanderings of the mind.

Lord Krishna has in mind the above situation when He gives guidance to the sadhak in the Bhagavad-Gita.

"One whose intelligence is established in the Divine abandons both good and evil. Therefore, Arjuna, devote yourself to yoga. Yoga is skill in action." (Chapter 2, verse 50)

The sadhak who has surrendered himself to the Lord should not think of the good or evil nature of any action performed by prana during meditation. He should strive to maintain a high level of meditation. In the above stanza, Lord Krishna has called the yogi, "the one whose intelligence is established in the Divine."

The Lord, Himself, lends clarity to this elsewhere by saying,

"Oh, Arjuna, during yogic meditation, perform all acts with a sense of detachment, without concern for achievements or failures, because the equanimity of intellect is itself called yoga." (Bhagavad-Gita, chapter 2, verse 48)

As long as the sadhak is affected by happiness when faced with success or by sorrow when faced with failure, his mind doesn't become detached. The perfection of yoga depends on detachment. This detachment isn't possible without the sense of self-sacrifice, or complete surrender to the Lord.

Notes to Myself

July 27th
(Tears of Separation)

I am 68 years old. I was 19 when I met my Reverend Gurudev. Forty-eight years have passed since then. When I observe the beautiful colors at the sunset of my life, my eyes fill with tears. These tears are tears of separation. After I met my holy Gurudev, I still had to live in the world. And even after my sanyas initiation (becoming a swami), I still had to live in the world. My ignorant self didn't know at that time that the world wasn't outside of me, but was within my own mind.

visianinfo.com

Notes to Myself

July 29th
(The Need for Tapas)

Before we can experience the Sadguru, we must perform tapas, or spiritual disciplines. A jeweler must study gems for a long time before he can tell the difference between a fake and a real gemstone, and even more years of tapas are required to know the jewel of the guru. The Sadguru can only be known through tapas. There's no doubt about this.

Muktidam in the original Kripalu Yoga Ashram in Sumneytown, Pennylvania where Bapuji did sadhana from 1977-1981. Photo by John Mundahl, 2007. Muktidam is now a shrine.

245

July 30th)
(If I Could, I Would Stay Here Forever)

In Sumneytown where I am living, it is extremely beautiful. I live on top of a hill. Even though such beauty is common in America, the natural setting where I live would delight the heart and eyes of anyone. My house is called Muktidham (house of liberation). It is a totally secluded place with a thick forest and many tall trees all around. It is completely tranquil. Sometimes deer walk by. A small garden around the house adds even more beauty. This is a proper place for yoga sadhana and I like it very much. I want to do nothing but yoga sadhana. I have no interest in any other activities. Since this is a foreign country, I have to obtain permission from the government again and again if I want to stay. If this were not a problem, I would not go anywhere else. I would pretend that this is Uttarkashi, a small town on the banks of the Ganges River, 8000 feet high in the Himalayas, and I would stay here permanently.

Muktidam in Sumneytown, Pennsylvania where Bapuji did sadhana from 1977-1981. Photo by John Mundahl, 2007.

246

July 31st
(True Sanyas is Death)

After someone dies, he's taken to a cemetery. He never returns from there. That is true sanyas, the renunciation of everything in the world. Sadhana is also death, so the place of sadhana is also like a cemetery. It's a place where the old you dies and doesn't return.

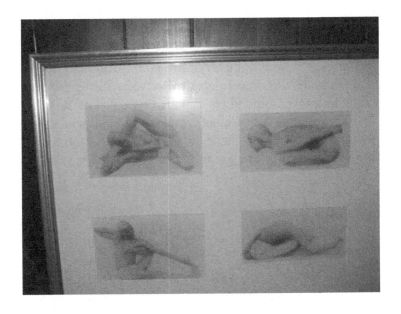

Photos of Bapuji doing spontaneous postures in India, circa 1955. These photos are from his book, *Asana and Mudra*, and are in Muktidam where he did his sadhana while visiting the United States from 1977-1981. This photo was taken by John Mundahl in 2007.

August

August 1st
(The Scriptures are the Friends of All)

When we are suffering, we turn to the scriptures and reflect upon them. The final realizations of the great masters of India are collected in the scriptures. We can read them and decide for ourselves if God exists. If we decide that God exists, we can consider His form. What is He, She or It like? If we decide that God doesn't exist, we can consider other questions. Where did everything come from and how is it sustained? We can find out if anyone in the past has come to know God and we can also receive comfort, joy, inspiration and knowledge from the great souls who thought deeply about these questions. The scriptures are the friends of all. They represent God.

www.mayapur.com

Bapuji teaching in the United States at the original Kripalu Yoga Retreat in Summit Station, Pennsylvania, 1978.   Photo from archives of Umesh Eric Baldwin.

August 2nd
(In Order to Recognize Greatness, We Must be Great)

Until unity exists between guru and disciple, they don't know each other. A disciple becomes capable, or worthy, of receiving the Sadguru only after accumulating much good karma from numerous lifetimes. If a disciple receives the Sadguru before that, he won't experience total reverence for him or be able to measure the depth of knowledge, detachment and greatness of the Sadguru. In order to recognize knowledge, we must have knowledge. In order to recognize detachment, we must be detached. In order to recognize greatness, we must be great.

Notes to Myself

250

Bapuji arriving for darshan, winter, 1978, Summit Station, Pennsylvania. Photo from archives of Umesh Eric Baldwin. Swami Vinit Muni is on the left in the picture.

August 3rd
(The Day My Mother Became My Disciple

One time in a village in India the members of the spiritual fellowship extended a special invitation to my mother and she stayed there happily for a few days. While returning home, she shyly said to me,

"Swamiji." She reverently called me swamiji because I had been initiated as a renunciate. "Now I'm old and can't follow you around wherever you go. If you come home to Dabhoi just one night a year, I'll be content."

I affectionately gave my consent.

About a year later I was on my way to Rajpipila. Suddenly I remembered the promise I had made to my mother as I approached Dabhoi, which was in the same direction. I walked home and it was lunchtime. My mother was performing her daily puja. She was overjoyed to see me, but continued her worship until she was finished.

Ten minutes later, carrying a ceremonial tray, she came gently toward where I was sitting. She sat down in front of me and I was surprised. I didn't know what she was going to do.

"Extend both of your feet," she said, in the sweet voice of a young girl.

"My feet?" I asked. I was sitting cross-legged in the chair. "Why?"

"I want to wash your feet. Today I want mantra initiation from you. I want you for my guru. I have great faith in you, for you have never deceived me. My husband was a devotee of the Lord and both of my sons

252

are renunciates. Now, like a solitary tree standing in the desert, I'm all alone in this world. I want to pass the rest of my life in devotion to the Lord. Swamiji, please briefly give me guidance so that I'll die in peace. I've spent all these years without a guru, just to meet you, the Sadguru. I'm illiterate and foolish, but I have faith that you'll take me to the opposite shore."

Her throat was so choked with emotion that she could no longer speak. Although Mother had always tolerated pain well and rarely cried, she was crying profusely now. Each word had pierced my heart for I had never felt her speak so soulfully. During my youth, she generally spoke little and would mostly listen, since her husband and sons had dominant temperaments.

My eyes overflowed with tears and I stood up and embraced her. Now I saw her greatness and I realized that the mothers of the saints of ancient India must have been this simple, affectionate, and religion-loving.

I bowed down at her feet and sobbed,

"Mother, you've spoken so beautifully. But you're *my* guru! You shouldn't speak this way. *You* have inspired *me*, and *you're* the boat that takes everyone to the opposite shore. A boat doesn't need another boat. You don't need me to take your boat to the opposite shore."

My words had no impact on her at all.

"Do you still consider me to be your mother?" She asked, "Even after being initiated as a swami?"

"Of course," I said. "How could I forget to honor you as my mother? You're an extraordinarily special mother. You fed me, not just with your milk, but with liberation itself."

"Give me mantra initiation, then," she said firmly. "Just as you have initiated others." She had reached her final decision, so I sat back down. I knew the discussion was over.

Then she washed my feet with great love. After puja, I gave her mantra initiation with the proper guidance.

Finally, she reverently bowed down to me and offered me one and a quarter rupees as homage to her guru. Then she fed me the foods that I liked the most.

Whenever I remember this special event, I drown in the depths of my mother's greatness.

Bapuji's mother.
Photo from archives
of Umesh Eric Baldwin.

(Story from, "From The Heart of the Lotus, the Teaching Stories of Swami Kripalu," by John Mundahl. Monkfish Books, Rhinebeck, New York 2008)

August 4th
(The Temples of the Yogis)

A temple is a building with a statue in it, but it isn't just a museum with attractive sculptures. A temple is a stone scripture in which the secrets of yoga are inscribed. Temples are sculptured in the language of samadhi. Its language is symbolic and can be understood only by advanced yogis. The temples constructed by advanced yogis are encyclopedias of spiritual knowledge. The temples created by rich, worldly people are predominantly sculpture. They don't embody yogic secrets, although they may be exceptionally beautiful. For example, the Taj Mahal is a stunning work of art that millions enjoy, but it contains no yogic secrets.

www.youtube.com

Ganesha, Pashupatinath Hindu Temple, Kathmandu, Nepal. Photo
by Umesh Eric Baldwin.

256

August 5th
(The High Saints are the Foundation of the World)

The high saints are the foundation of the world. Such a person is a representative of God and can be called an embodiment of God because he, or she, is without ego. They have accepted the greatness of the Lord. They are the Ganges of sacred knowledge and a place of great pilgrimage. They bring holiness to all places of worship and for that reason can be called a *Tirthankar* (sacred pilgrimage site). Those who bathe in their holiness become saints. Those who drink their knowledge find happiness, satisfaction and peace. Such high saints are the foundation of the world. They are saviors who liberates us from the cycle of birth and death. Those who praise and worship them and follow their teachings are satsangis, sadhaks, disciples, seekers and devotees.

www.allindiaflorist.com

257

August 6th
(The Infallible Way to Happiness)

Love has two characteristics…surrender and service. Just as whiteness, liquidity and sweetness are inseparable from milk, surrender and service are inseparable from love. Living for a beloved person or for others is the infallible way to happiness. The subtle meaning of this is that the one we love is another form of ourselves, because love means the surrender of ourselves to another. We may call this "entering the body of another," because we enter the heart of our beloved and he or she enters our heart. This is love. Surrender and service to each other then become invisible.

Photo from archives of Umesh Eric Baldwin. 1980.

258

August 7th
(A Lonely Love)

Love for God is last. A fraction exists in most of us, however, and it's usually awakened during times of unhappiness. Love for God also is awakened when worldly love can't satisfy us anymore and we intuitively believe that there must be an eternal, true love or union. This divine realization places us on the spiritual path. It's described as a "lonely" form of love because we no longer have attachments for things of the world.

www.emaze.com
Notes to Myself

259

August 8th
(Divine Love)

Divine love resides beneath the countless layers in the heart. It cannot be experienced at once. When that auspicious moment arrives, the layers of the ego are put aside, the heart opens completely and we experience the fantastic taste of the divinity of love. The ego prevents surrender and service, but in divine love there is no "you" and "me." There exists only "thou." Attached lovers experience "you" and "me," and thus their love is incomplete.

hdhut.blogspot.com

260

August 9th
(Sanatan Dharma)

anatan Dharma says, *Vasudeva Kutumbakam,* "The whole world is one family." Love is God, dharma, Holy Scripture, knowledge, yoga and devotion. All of this exists in the family. Love is the basis of Pravritti Dharma and the family is the great purifying place for love. The great temple of Nivritti Dharma is then established on this foundation. The entire world is included in Nivritti Dharma. In other words, a seeker must first develop strong feelings for his family system and then these feelings of love are extended to the entire world. Thus, the scriptures say that dharma is born in the heart and it radiates out from there.

Notes to Myself

August 10th
(The Vishnu Mantra)

You all chant the Vishnu mantra, *Om Namo Bhagavate Vasudevaya*, to purify your mind and body. Be sure to repeat it sincerely. If you practice this japa in the best possible way, you will purify your body and mind, and the feeling of surrender will flourish in you. This mantra, and others such as Gayatri, Ram, and Om, are mantras of divine origin. They have all evolved from anahat nad. The simple letters, words, and sentences which form these mantras aren't as simple as they seem. They have special energy hidden in them and grant wonderful blessings to the seeker.

Notes to Myself

August 11th
(We Cannot Live without Each Other)

If there was only one person on earth, that person wouldn't know the joy of life, because he wouldn't have anyone to love. We can't live without each other. We need each other. We are always looking for those we can trust and truly share our hearts. We have a beautiful flower in our hands to accomplish this. It's the flower of love, our ability to love. Poets call this our heart. We offer our heart to someone. To enter the heart of another is to forget our ego. This is the offering. This is the surrender. It's the grand experiment of our existence. We are born to love each other. What a beautiful way to purify our ego.

www.pinterest.com

August 12th
(There is no Hesitation in True Love)

True love is just an offering. It doesn't expect something in return. There is no hesitation in true love, because it doesn't expect anything back. That is the principle of love. It's a free will offering. It's not an exchange. There's no begging. The experiment should first be carried out in the family. Then, after many incarnations, we give this love to God and Guru. A true Guru is an ocean of love. He or she expects or asks nothing of anyone. This person is capable of loving us as a father, mother, brother, sister, friend, even as a child. I experienced such a Guru. I was looking for someone who I could completely give my life to and by the grace of God, I found such a person. After that, my disillusionment with life turned to joy. He modeled the saintly life to me and gave me the strength to seek it for myself.

www.mauigoose.com

264

August 13th
(The Aspirations of our Heart)

It's a great fortune and a blessing to find a true Guru. The aspirations of our heart are nurtured then, not lost, and we come to understand love. Sometimes we receive love from others only when we offer them love first, but the Guru's love is offered to us freely. We don't have to do anything. Can someone get love from a Guru without being a disciple, then? Does the Guru really love everyone? Why, then, does it seem that he loves the disciple best? When it rains, water flows naturally from high spots into low spots. We could say that the low spots are ready to receive the rainwater. In the same way, a humble person is ready to receive the Guru. So, some preparation is needed on our part to receive the Guru's love and knowledge. It's true that when we give love, we receive love. It appears to be an exchange, but it isn't. Love doesn't look at itself. It always looks at the other. It naturally loses itself in whatever it loves. Peace, joy and happiness spring from this union.

Notes to Myself

August 14th
(Try to Bring Joy to Others)

Going to the guru is like going to the dentist. Once you get there, the ache goes away. We all carry this ache. It is the ache of suffering. The ache is relieved by love, so become a dentist and extend your love to those around you. Try to bring joy to others, especially those people you live with. Sit down together and determine that you will bring happiness to each other. Then you, too, can be happy and when you're happy it's easy to love.

www.awesomelycute.com

266

August 15th
(Love *is* the sadhana)

Love *is* the sadhana. So, in your rush to perfect a posture, don't miss the obvious. Remember to love. If you sit in front of God in your meditation room with a long face, what can God do with you? Your meditation room may be filled with flowers, incense and holy pictures, but if your heart is closed, it doesn't matter.

Photo from archives of Umesh Eric Baldwin. 1979.

August 16th
(Wherever a Lamp Goes)

Wherever a lamp goes, it spreads light. Wherever a flower goes, it spreads fragrance. Wherever we go, we should spread love. We are devotees of God and God is love. We don't have to say, "I love you," to everyone. Just be kind, patient, tolerant, forgiving and soft-spoken. This is the love adored by God.

Bapuji in his darshan room in Muktidam in the United States in 1978. Photo from archives of Umesh Eric Baldwin.

August 17th
(Truth Belongs to All)

Long ago, people asked the spiritual masters: "I'm not happy. There's no peace and joy in my life. What can I do to relieve the restlessness, pain and sorrow in my mind?" So the great masters studied this situation deeply. They had no intention of starting a religion. They were simply spiritual explorers. And when they discovered a great spiritual Truth, they gave it freely to the world. "*Satya*" or "Truth," they said, "Doesn't belong to any particular nation or individual. It belongs to all." So the great masters had no interest in converts or developing a large following. They didn't even put their names to the scriptures they wrote. Their only interest was the moral development of mankind. Just as the automobile, television or airplane can be used by anyone, so too, the discoveries of these great souls can be used by anyone.

Notes to Myself

August 18th
(The Two Paths of Sanatan Dharma)

Sanatan Dharma, the eternal religion of India, has two paths. Nivritti Dharma is the dharma of liberation. It is for great souls such as Maharishi Vyasa, Maharishi Patanjali, Divarishi Narad, Maharishi Vishwamitra and Maharishi Lakulish. In this dharma, the kundalini force is awakened fully and aspirants withdrew from society and practice intense kundalini yoga for their entire life. The other dharma is Pravriti Dharma, or social religion. If is for those living and working in society and for those having a family. The purpose of the two dharmas is the same, purification and moral upliftment, but the means are different. Pravriti Dharma is detailed. There are guidelines for parents, children, relatives, husband, wife, son, daughter, guest, host, student, teacher, friendship, how to talk, eat, worship, pray, chant, marry and so forth. A loving family life is extremely important, so householders are taught to practice tolerance, patience, acceptance, forgiveness and worship of God, both at home in a ceremony called puja and in the temples.

www.windowssearch-exp.com

270

August 19th
(Sahaj Yoga)

The Muladhara chakra and the Swadhisthana chakra are related to each other. The apana vayu rules these two regions. There is a collection of 72,000 nadis (bodily passages) in the region of the apana vayu. Without the help of kundalini, the purification of these nadis isn't possible.

To achieve the purification of these nadis is like crossing the Vaitarani River, a river that is said in the Puranas to be situated between Mrtyuloka (earth) and Yamaloka (the other world). It is full of hot blood, bones and hair. People flounder in this river, unable to swim across it.

Holy people swim across it by holding on to a cow's tail. Yogis consider the body, filled with blood, bones and hair as the Vaitarani River. They use the cow's tail, in the form of kundalini, to cross the river and become immortal.

It is better to die once while living with a smiling face than to die thousands of times crying and unwilling. To die a living death means to surrender oneself to God and to sacrifice oneself at His lotus feet.

Notes to Myself

Bapuji doing spontaneous mudras, part of the manifestations of Sahaj Yoga. 1978, while in the United States. Photo from archives of Umesh Eric Baldwin.

August 20th
(The Gift of Self-Observation)

I have observed silence for 18 years. What benefit did I get from doing this? There are many benefits and it could be the topic of an entire talk, but I will tell you one gem that I received. *The gift of self-observation.* Whenever I behave improperly during the day, it causes me suffering in my sadhana. Deep self-observation happens automatically during my sadhana and my mistake comes running to me. It just jumps out right in front of me, even though I may have completely overlooked it during the day. To me this is a wonderful grace, because this is how I grow. Without this special gift, my life wouldn't be what it is today. So, self-observation is a tremendous benefit of silence. Another, of course, is that we become more aware of our speech, that is, we develop more control over what we say and how we say it.

Notes to Myself

Bapuji's writing desk inside Muktidam. Photo by John Mundahl, 2007.

August 21st
(We Want Peace)

We want peace, but we aren't willing to be silent. We speak much more than necessary. Our bitter words result in quarrels. When gentle people speak, it's like a bottle of perfume has opened. When arrogant people speak, it's like a foul-smelling sewer has opened. When you speak, be sure you are opening a bottle of perfume and not a sewer.

www.1000funfacts.com

Today I will be conscious of my speech.

August 22nd
(The Sacred Pilgrimage Sites)

The glory of sacred pilgrimage sites is well known and people have taken these pilgrimages for thousands of years. If people didn't receive benefit from them, these pilgrimages would have diminished long ago. Yet, even in this modern era this hasn't happened. This is evidence enough that this activity is meaningful, not useless. Naturally, not everyone receives the same benefit from such a pilgrimage because each person differs, but everyone experiences to some degree the divine energy that exists in such a holy place and this satisfies him or her to some degree.

The Temple built by the people in Kayavarohan, India, under Bapuji's supervision to honor Lord Brameshwar. Photo by Umesh Eric Baldwin in 1981.

August 23rd
(Why do Swamis Establish Ashrams?)

The ashram is also a special place of pilgrimage. Not only is it different from the other sacred sites, it's the best, because it's a holy place of knowledge, religion, tapas and culture. Usually ashrams are established by great acharyas who are swamis. If swamis have renounced their old home, why do they start a new one? Isn't an ashram a home, also? True swamis have no need for either homes or ashrams. It's their benevolence that leads them to establish ashrams for the welfare of others.

In India, circa 1945. Photo from archives of Umesh Eric Baldwin.

277

August 24th
(You Will Have to Practice This)

We should speak kindly, in a way that doesn't cause pain to anyone, or speak less, or observe silence. This is Sanatan Dharma, remembering our connection to everyone. It is the immortal religion, the religion that knows no nationality or border. It is the religion of God. You will have to practice this. Our tongue loves sweet food, yet spews forth bitter food. Be careful. We know how to speak pleasantly, but we forget. However, once we firmly decide to practice this sadhana, God will help us.

Kind words are sweet to the soul

Speak Kindness

Speak Sweetness

Speak Love...

JollyNotes.com magnet sample

www.jollynotes.com

Notes to Myself

August 25th
(Suffering Fills the Holes in our Colander)

As long as we are attracted to the world, as long as we like the sensual delights, spiritual knowledge can be put in our lap and we will walk away from it or not recognize it. But when we decide that we've had enough, when we begin to walk away from the attractions of the world by our own willpower, by conscious choice, then we begin to receive spiritual knowledge. We begin to recognize and value its importance. As long as our mind is the victim of the temptations of the world, we won't experience the in-depth failure, the suffering and pain needed to drive us unto the spiritual path. If you dip a colander into the river, you won't come up with any water. The mind of a worldly man can't hold spiritual knowledge because it's like a colander. Arjuna, in the opening chapter of the Bhagavad Gita, is at this point. His suffering is deep. He sees no way out. It's at this point that we turn to God. Suffering fills the holes in our colander and we become capable of holding the spiritual water, the knowledge.

Notes to Myself

August 26th
(The Beginning of the Bhagavad Gita)

In order to contact God, we must cut off those things that disturb our mind. Gradually, we develop non-attachment to the world of the senses because little by little, through pain, through touching the hot flame, we know that it leads to suffering. But this takes a long time, many, many incarnations, until we finally completely give up and turn away from the things of the world and become Arjuna. That is where Arjuna is in his spiritual walk as the Bhagavad Gita begins. He has completely given up. He's to the point of either suicide or sincerely stepping upon the spiritual path, which is suicide, too, gradual suicide, the death of the ego. The person we thought we were dies daily on the spiritual path.

Bapuji meditating in the United States, 1977. Photo from archives of Umesh Eric Baldwin.

August 27th
(Arriving at the End of it All)

Most of us feel bad for a while and then good for a while. We cry a little bit at life and then we laugh a little bit. As long as we are still in this state, we are not like Arjuna in the Bhagavad Gita. Arjuna had totally arrived at the end of it all. Shouldn't we laugh and enjoy life, then? Yes, laughter and joy should be part of living, but we should be laughing at our own foolishness, then the yoga of Arjuna can begin. Think of an archer. Before he releases his arrow, he becomes totally focused, totally concentrated and one-pointed, and then he releases his arrow. Arjuna, now, is like that archer. This condition of deep despair and disappointment is a special condition. It is highly prized by the great masters. They examine their disciples carefully to see if that condition is there. That is the condition that creates readiness for spiritual knowledge. It allows us to focus our minds completely on the teachings.

Notes to Myself

Winter, 1979. Photo from archives of Umesh Eric Baldwin.

August 28th
(This Allows the Knowledge to Flow)

Seekers who understand the value of knowledge understand the value of the guru. If we don't truly understand the value of knowledge, we aren't ready for the guru. There may be 25 pots of water on a table, but if you aren't thirsty, what good are they? If you don't have the thirst for knowledge, what good is the guru who is a pot full of water? So, first we must have a thirst for knowledge. When this thirst becomes intense, the search for a guru happens automatically. Then we should prepare ourselves to receive the teachings. What good is a beautiful instrument in the hands of a child? Likewise, you may find a high guru, but if you aren't ready to receive the teachings, what good is the guru to you? So, preparation is part of the thirst for knowledge, too. Then you must have love for the guru. You may find a guru, but if the love isn't there, the knowledge won't flow toward you. When there is love, the heart of the seeker is wide open and the seeker wants to be near the guru, wants to serve the guru, wants to be close to the guru. The scriptures of India say that one will attain the higher knowledge only in service to the guru. The flame of love must be burning in the heart of the seeker. As long as this flame isn't lit, there is no desire to serve the guru properly. With love, comes the desire to serve. From service comes surrender. Surrender of what? Our ego. Now love is complete. Our actions are now *sattvic,* pure, and this allows the knowledge to flow.

283

August 29th
(The Great Mahatmas of India Need Nothing)

Does a guru need service and does he only teach when he is loved, then? No, there's no selfish motive on the part of the guru. It's in the interest of the seeker to serve, not in the interest of the guru. Who can truly serve? Only those who are capable can serve. The rich can serve the poor. The educated can serve the illiterate. Those with sight can serve the blind. Those who can walk can serve a cripple. A guru doesn't need service. The great Mahatmas of India need nothing. How can we serve such a person, then? The service we give them is only ordinary. The seeker does whatever he can to stay close to the guru...washes a dish, fills a water pot, cooks a meal. Once a piece of cotton touches perfume, however, it smells like perfume. This is the result of contact. Now tell me, did the cotton serve the perfume or did the perfume serve the cotton?

www.atthefeetof the guru.com

284

August 30
(Putting on the New)

To serve means *to be close to.* This isn't as easy as it sounds. It isn't easy to do what the guru likes, to do *only* those things that the guru likes. What does the guru like? He likes good character. He is constantly asking us to change, to drop our old ways and put on the new and this is difficult. Here we fight. Here we need love. Love starts with service and moves to surrender. Surrender of what? Our ego. Now we can change. Now we can stop fighting and put on the new.

www.epicdogtraining.net

Notes to Myself

August 31st
(The Miracle of Sod)

The purpose of yoga is to attain happiness, peace and bliss, not yogic powers or to demonstrate miracles. What is a miracle? A miracle is a surprise, something we don't understand. America is a land of great physical sciences. To me, it's full of miracles, full of surprises. I'm from India and have never seen many of the things that are commonplace for you. When I was first introduced to my new home in Summit Station at Amrit's ashram, there was no grass in the back yard. Two days later, the back yard was full of beautiful, green grass! What's this, I thought? How did this happen? And then someone told me about the miracle of sod.

Photo from archives of Umesh Eric Baldwin. 1979.

286

September

September 1st,
(Yogic Miracles)

Yoga was born in India. Since you live in America, you're unfamiliar with the culture and history of India. Small children know about yoga and the powers of yogis and they accept these things without surprise. Yoga is now coming to your country and you should know that if you approach yoga with the hope of attaining yogic powers, it will lead you down the wrong path. Those who want to create miracles should remain as physical scientists, not as spiritual scientists, not as yogis.

Notes to Myself

Photo from archives of Umesh Eric Baldwin. Summer, 1977.

September 2nd
(Why Do You Want To See a Yogi Fly?)

Surprises and miracles won't captivate our mind forever. When the airplane, radio, submarine, telephone and television were invented, people were spellbound. Yet, within a short time these things were commonplace. Likewise, if yogis fly in the sky to satisfy the curiosity of society, it would cause a great stir at first. But then, once you had seen it, the interest would wane. Who would want to stand for days with upturned eyes and watch a yogi fly in the sky? Aren't you busy people with better things to do? And we would have to be far from airports, wouldn't we, so we didn't crash into airplanes? I'm being funny on purpose. But really, why should we use the precious years of our life to learn to fly? What purpose does that serve? Baby birds learn to fly within a few days. A seeker would have to spend many, many years or lifetimes mastering this skill. Do you want to be a bird or do you want to be a yogi? Please think about this. Yes, the scriptures of India say that yogis can fly, but yogis don't seek this power. It comes automatically as they progress in yoga and they hide this achievement because it has no use to them or to society.

Notes to Myself

September 3rd
(Yogic Miracles)

L et's consider the airplane for a moment. Someone looked at a bird and thought, *I wish I could do that.* So scientists got together and invented the airplane, even though they themselves couldn't fly. To most of us who don't understand the laws of physics, it's almost a miracle, an airplane weighing thousands and thousands of pounds can float like a feather through the air! How wonderful! And because of that miracle, millions and millions of people each day now take sky journeys. What a wonderful invention for the benefit of humanity! So, is it better to observe a yogi flying through the air while you're standing on the ground, or is it better to observe a yogi standing on the ground while you're flying through the air? I presume you would prefer the latter. An event may be dramatic, such as a yogi flying through the air, but it isn't worth much if it doesn't benefit others.

www.theinquirer.net.

September 4th
(Walking on Water)

Another yogic power is the ability to walk on water. Ducks can walk on water. Even their babies can do this shortly after birth. And yet everyone wants to see a yogi walk on water. And for what purpose? How does this help anyone? When I was in Summit Station at Amrit's ashram, he told me that the small lake nearby froze in the wintertime and the disciples walked and skated on the ice. Are Amrit's disciples high yogis, then? They can walk on water! If a person drowns, his body floats on water. Yet, everyone wants to see a yogi walk on water. Scientists invented the boat so we can *all* walk on water and look how this invention has helped our lives.

www.howtocopewithpain.org

291

September 5th
(Hearing from a Distance)

A Siddha yogi can overhear a conversation thousands of miles away. So what? How does this help anyone? We can turn the radio on and do the same thing. A Siddha yogi can also see things thousands of miles away. So what? How does this help anyone? We can turn on the television and do the same thing. All miracles are created by God, even the inventions of the physical world. These inventions come from God through the mind of the scientist who brings the invention into the world for the benefit of many. The miracles of spiritual masters come from God, too, through the spiritual master into the world for a specific purpose, maybe a healing. In both cases, man is merely the instrument. The only difference is that a spiritual miracle should be used more discreetly. And even that isn't correct because spiritual miracles happen automatically by the will of God through the body and mind of the yogi. The yogi doesn't plan these things. That would involve ego and he has given his ego to God.

Notes to Myself

September 6th
(Forget About Miracles)

You are all on the yogic path. Don't get sidetracked by yogic powers. They are useless to a true yogi. The yogi has to give them all up in the end, anyway. The purpose of the spiritual path is to perfect your character, not to amaze others with yogic powers. The two feet of the Beloved Lord are right conduct and self-control. Forget about miracles and grasp these two feet firmly.

Photo from archives of Umesh Eric Baldwin. 1980

September 7th
(Two Kinds of Teachers)

There are two kinds of teachers. The first kind teaches a subject in school. The second kind is a spiritual teacher. The word in Sanskrit for the second kind is *acharya*. It means one who has progressed on the spiritual path and now is teaching. Sometimes we use the word *dharmacharya*, or teachers of dharma. The first teacher teaches a subject. They want their students to master a certain body of knowledge. The second teacher teaches character. They want their students to master their character. The first teacher should be a master of their particular subject and the second teacher should be a master of their character.

Speech to 25,000 people in 1971, Kayavarohan, India. Coming out of 12 years of silence. Photo from archives of Umesh Eric Baldwin.

September 8th
(The Acharya)

There is a vast difference between a five thousand dollar bill and a five dollar bill, even though the two are the same size and both made of paper. The *acharya* is like the five thousand dollar bill. Don't be discouraged by this. You can all become *acharyas*, but it happens in stages, one step at a time. A sculptor begins with raw stone. Little by little, he carves a beautiful statue, but it takes time and effort. The masterpiece at the end of spiritual effort is the acharya.

www.flickr.com

Notes to Myself

295

September 9th
(Sahaj Yoga)

Lord Shiva says in Shiva Samhita,
"Shaktichalana mudra is that mudra in which the wise sadhak should capture the apana and forcibly attract the dormant kundalini power to ascend. Thus, this all-powerful mudra when practiced destroys all diseases and lends longevity to life. Its practice awakens the kundalini and makes it ascendant. Therefore, those yogis who aspire for miraculous powers should practice this mudra. By its practice, the body is purified and the eight major miraculous powers, including the power of becoming microscopic like an atom are achieved." (Shiva Samhita, chapter 4, verses 105-108)

It is said in Hathayoga Pradipika,
"One who has been able to accord movement to shakti (power) is entitled to achieve miraculous powers. What more can be said? He can miraculously attain immortality." (Hathayoga Pradipika, verse 120)

In Gheranda Samhita it is said,
"He who regularly practices shaktichalana mudra attains divine body purified by yogic fire. He achieves miraculous powers and all the diseases in his body are destroyed." (Gheranda Samhita, chapter 3, verse 60)

Bapuji doing spontaneous mudras, a manifestation in Sahaj Yoga. 1978. Kripalu Yoga Retreat, Summit Station, Pennsylvania. Photo from archives of Umesh Eric Baldwin.

September 10th
(Satsanga)

Satsanga has two homes. One home is found by reading scripture. The other is found by being with saints. Through contact with these two, we clearly see our faults and progress closer to God. One who finds a high saint has truly received the grace and blessings of the Lord. This contact brings peace of mind and knowledge of sadhana. How can we practice sadhana without knowledge? Just as we need money to start a business, we need knowledge to start sadhana.

Bapuji in the United States. Summer, 1977. Photo from archives of Umesh Eric Baldwin.

298

September 11th
(Why Does Our Journey Take so Long?)

By the grace of the guru, or saint, we attain a higher consciousness, and by the grace of the Lord we attain a guru. Both are connected and when we reach the Lord, our life is fulfilled. Our journey ends. Why does the journey take so long? Because we come to the saint with lots of bad company. Our bad company is our destructive thoughts, in other words, our disturbed mind.

Photo from Vandita Kate Marchesiello.

Today my prayer is…

September 12th
(Guidance from my Guru)

Now I will give you, in short, the guidance my beloved Guru gave to me:

1. Accept that God exists and that there is only one God.

2. Practice yama and niyama to the best of your ability.

3. Pray to God and repeat mantra and japa.

4. Speak loving, but keep silent as much as possible.

5. Eat moderately, one nourishing meal a day, fast one day a week.

6. Do asana, pranayam and meditation according to your capacity.

7. Study the scriptures, especially the books written by your Guru.

8. Keep the company of saints.

9. Practice right action, sensual restraint, self-analysis and faithfully perform your duties.

Notes to Myself

September 13th
(Sanatan Dharma)

You like to wear Indian clothes. You have Sanskrit names. You like the Indian lifestyle. Then you must like the Indian religion, too. That religion is called Sanatan Dharma, the immortal religion. The religion cannot be destroyed because truth cannot be destroyed. Only truth is immortal. Everything else is destructible. The great yogis discovered the truth of the soul and called it Sanatan Dharma. This religion was born in sacred places in the woods and has been sustained by sacred pilgrimage places called *tirthas*. It isn't a religious sect. It contains the supreme potential of man. So the yogis never had any need to propagate it. Nobody has ever desired to do missionary work for Sanatan Dharma. Furthermore, the great masters who realized this truth and who wrote the scriptures, never even wrote their name after what they wrote, because they didn't consider it to be theirs.

www.slideshare.net

301

September 14th
(Chanting OM)

Usually, sound begins with thought. We think of what we want to say and then we say it or sing it out loud. In Kundalini Yoga, mantra yoga happens automatically when prana and apana join together and rise up from the base of the spine. The yogi chants Ram or OM automatically. This is called spontaneous sound, or *anahat nad,* or unstruck sound. The OM sound actually contains three sounds A-U-M and sounds like this when it's chanted spontaneously:

(Bapuji chants the AUM sound).

When prana moves through the *visuddha chakra,* the throat chakre, the sound of AUM is produced. Prana then moves into *ajna chakra,* the chakra in the forehead, and the AUM sound changes a bit. It sounds like this:

(Bapuji chants AUM again).

Notice the "M" is prolonged. There is more of a humming sound and not so much of the "Ah" sound.

www.chikriyoga.com

302

September 15th
(The Tracks of Religion)

If a train doesn't run on tracks, it will have an accident. Likewise, if we don't run on the tracks of religion, we will have an accident, too, a moral accident. Don't let that happen to you. Let your life be guided by the tracks of religion. This isn't easy to do. It's difficult. It's easy only if you love it. If you love it, you won't wrestle with it and make it hard.

Notes to Myself

September 16th
(How to Chant OM)

Before you chant OM, you must relax and withdraw the energy, the outgoing energy, and focus it within. Then take a long, deep breath and chant the sound of OM. Continue to say OM as long as you can with one breath. Then experience the vibrations that are generated within your body and mind. Start another OM and let your mind dissolve in the sound. Then sit still and experience the vibrations generated within your body and mind again. If you continue doing this with a peaceful, steady mind, you will experience peace, joy, and bliss. OM chanting is beautiful, very powerful. Practice like this and it will help you. OM is the highest mantra. It is the king mantra. All the other mantras are included in it.

www.flickr.com

304

September 17th
(The Root Source of Thought)

Thoughts emerge from our mouth as spoken language. Spoken language is called *mudyama* in Sanskrit. But language first exists in our mind as subtle speech, or thoughts, speech without an alphabet. This is called *pasenji* in Sanskrit. The language of *pasenji* doesn't reveal itself as speech until the thoughts are completely formed. Then there is the language of *parawani*. This is the root source of *pasenji*. In other words, this is the root source of thought. When a yogi arrives here, he is close to God. He is in touch with Cosmic Consciousness. The great sounds like Ram and OM and the immortal mantras of India that the yogi chants in sadhana come from *parawani* and thus from God. Sanskrit is so beautiful because it has words for all of these things. That is why it is called the language of the Gods. At the level of *parawani*, the subtlest level, there is only the language of Truth. There is no distortion here, no pollution. I'm speaking to you this morning through this loudspeaker, which makes my voice and words clear. In the same way, when God speaks to the meditating yogi in the *parawani* state of consciousness, it's like God using a loudspeaker. The words are clear with no distortion. The Bible and the other great scriptures of the world are from the *parawani* state of consciousness. Thus, the words are called scriptures and are meant to relieve people of suffering, to point the way to peace and happiness.

September 18th
(Our Dear Friend, Prana)

During the day, prana is active in our limbs accomplishing the work of the day. At night when we're asleep, prana is free to work on the inner level and it purifies us internally and heals us, especially when we are sick. That's why rest is so important when we are sick, because prana is free to heal us. Prana is our dear friend. It's too bad we don't know our friend very well. She is a friend who never rests. She is always working for us, either in the waking state or the sleep state. In the waking state, she does what our mind tells her to do. In the sleep state, she does what she wants to do, free of the demands of the mind. If our cells are worn out, she replaces them. She is happy when we sleep, because then she can do her most important work. When we take time to simply relax, prana is happy. It's like an extra blessing to her, because now she doesn't have to wait for us to fall asleep at night. She can move from our limbs and our active minds to re-establish our internal health. So, conscious relaxation is an important key to mental and physical health. It's an important thing to master. The key is to allow your mind to become a witness. Allow your thoughts to just come and go and don't feed them with your attention. Then prana is free to work internally.

Notes to Myself

September 19th
(The Essence of the Gita)

Our life should be guided by prana, prompted by prana, not our mind, which is subject to duality and the pain that comes with it. In kundalini sadhana, the seeker sits for meditation, ignites his prana, and then drops his mind and watches prana do all the actions. This is called Sahaj Yoga, natural yoga, or spontaneous yoga, and there is no karma from these actions because they come from God, prana, and not our mind, which is the instrument of ego. This is called *inaction in action* because there is no karma from these actions. Eventually, the yogi's mind becomes so purified by this sadhana that even when the yogi is mixing with the world again, his actions still come from prana because his mind is purified and it isn't a hindrance. Prana, God, is flowing cleaning through the yogi's mind and all external actions. So Krishna is saying, "Drop your ego." This is the essence of the Gita and the beautiful chapters tell us how to do that. It must be done in stages and those stages are called sadhana.

Notes to Myself

September 20th
(When We're Finished with Everything)

Lord Krishna says at the end of the Gita: "Come to
Me!" What he means by this is: Drop your ego.
Purify your ego. Become one with the energy of
the Lord. Become one with God. Then all suffering ends
and this is done through sadhana. The devotee of the
Lord firmly says, "I am not the performer of my actions.
The Lord, Himself, is directing my actions and I have
nothing to do with their results. Whatever the Lord
directs me to do through my body, mind, intellect and
consciousness, I will perform. It's all by His wish." This
means that his ego is so purified that there is no personal
desire left anymore. The devotee acts only in accordance
with God's will. After taking your seat in a boat, you
don't have to swim anymore. Only the boat swims. The
state of oneness with the Lord is like that and it's so
subtle, interesting and full of joy that it can hardly be
described. When I read the old scriptures of India my
eyes fill with tears. They are so beautiful. This union *is*
the life. When we're finished with everything, after
thousands and thousands of incarnations, we only have
one wish left, "My Lord, I want only You."

Notes to Myself

September 21st
(First Experience of Pranothana)

I had been doing *anuloma-viloma pranayam* (alternate nostril breathing) for about three months, three times a day for an hour in each sitting. Amrit was about fifteen, then, and I was staying in his town of Halol. My guru had taught me only *padmasana* (the lotus) and *anuloma-viloma.* Gradually, I increased my practice from three hours a day to five hours a day.

I was staying in a building that had cows and there were many mosquitoes. One day, I was doing *anuloma-viloma* with a mosquito net over my bed when my body suddenly lurched forward into *bhunamapadmasana* (a forward bending posture) and I went unconscious.

I don't remember how long I lay like that, but when I woke up I wondered what had happened to me. For my next sitting, I found a mat and put it on the floor and set my mosquito net aside. I was extremely curious about what had happened and I didn't want to be sitting on a bed under a mosquito net.

I started my pranayam and suddenly I stood up and started dancing! I was thrilled! Completely overjoyed! Indian dance is unique. No one thought it up or created it. It came from the yogis, from spontaneous prana in their sadhanas. My mind was totally captivated by all of this, filled with joy and wonder. The movements were so graceful and beautiful!

I didn't have a single book on yoga, nor had I read any books, so I left Halol and moved to a nearby town and compiled a list of all the yogic books. I wrote letters to the publishers and gathered all the books I could. The books I had previously read were philosophical (jnana yoga) and devotional (bhakti yoga), but I had read nothing on the yogic process itself (karma yoga).

My beloved Gurudev was so smart. He had told me only the most important information on yoga sadhana, nothing more, and yet he had given me everything worth knowing. But he had left all of the details up to me. These things I had to find out on my own.

Bapuji doing spontaneous postures, circa 1955. Photo from *Asana and Mudra* and archives of Umesh Eric Baldwin.

September 22nd
(Make Your Personal Life Beautiful)

First, make your personal life beautiful and pure. Imagine that there are thousands of candles arranged in front of you in a circle, but the candles are not lit, so it gets dark at night. But in the middle of all the candles there is one burning and that is you, your ability to bring love into this world, and from that one candle you can light all the other candles so the darkness goes away. One candle can light thousands. This is what great saints do and you can do that, too. Open your heart to the love of God and see what happens.

Notes to Myself

September 23rd
(Love is Seeking Us)

Love is seeking us, but can't find us. It enters our life when we examine our own character through self-awareness, when we honestly observe how loving we are and strive to change those parts of our character that aren't loving. Then love gives itself totally to the beloved. As long as we can't forget the external world, we can't truly enter the chamber of our heart, and as long as we fail to enter the inner chamber of our heart, self-observation isn't possible. When two people love each other, they become one. Love is a beautiful thing for these two people. It transforms their lives.

shareably.net

September 24th
(The Power of the Soul)

Whenever your mind wanders in the external world you dissipate energy. When you focus your attention within, you conserve energy. Self-observation, which is the internal focusing of our energy, renews our energy. It doesn't create more problems for us. You will get more energy. A tree with deeper roots has more capacity to grow. So when we focus our attention within, our energy goes within and we attain the strength or power of Atman, of soul, which is purity.

Photo from archives of Umesh Eric Baldwin. 1979.

September 25th
(When You Encounter a Problem)

Do your self-observation with love and have trust and faith in God. When you encounter a problem, drop the thought and start japa. Engage all your attention in mantra japa and pray like this: "Lord, you are the source of all strength. I turn to You now in my time of need." Just offer your problem to the Lord and be free from all worries and concerns. Know that the merciful Lord will do what is most appropriate for you. Brahmacharya is also helpful. Being secluded is helpful. Read inspiring books. Keep pictures of the great masters close by, those who inspire you. Their presence will give you strength and divine inspiration.

Notes to Myself

314

September 26th
(The Disciple Who Almost Drown)

There once was a man who was looking for a guru. He was a serious devotee, but he had not found a guru to his liking yet. He had visited many saints in India, but he had always left unsatisfied. His question to each saint was the same.

"How can I create a burning desire for God, one that will bring immediate results?"

No saint he visited could answer this question to his satisfaction. One day, by chance, Ramakrishna Paramahansa, the Guru of Swami Vivekenanda was near by. This devotee asked around and found Ramakrishna. He was walking next to a river.

"Kind, sir," the devotee asked sincerely. "How can I create a burning desire for God, one that will bring immediate results?"

"Son," Ramakrishna replied sweetly. "I can't give you that answer here on the bank of the river. But come with me into the water, and I can give it to you there."

"I will do that," the devotee replied. "I'll go with you."

Ramakrishna took the man's hand and gently led him into the river. Deeper and deeper they went. Then suddenly with great force, Ramakrishna pushed the man's head under the water and held it there and wouldn't let him up! The man struggled and kicked and drank water trying to breath. Finally, just before the man drown, Ramakrishna grabbed the man by his hair and pulled him up.

"Save me! Save me!" The man screamed. "I'm drowning!"

"That's a burning desire," Ramakrishna said sweetly. "We have to cry to God from deep pain, then God will save us." (*From, "From the Heart of the Lotus, the Teaching Stories of Swami Kripalu," by John Mundahl. Monkfish Books, Rhinebeck, New York 2008)*

Inside Muktidam. The steps to Bapuji's upstairs meditation room where he did sadhana from 1977-1981 while in the United States. Photo by John Mundahl in 2007

September 27th
(When We Exist Only as the Energy of God)

When I leave here today, I will sit in a car and I will "surrender myself to the car" and the car will move me. The car will take care of everything. I won't have to walk. Similarly, when we surrender our mind, consciousness, intellect, ego, body, everything to God, there is nothing else for us to do. We still must work and do our daily duties, but we do them as inspired by God. Our ego life is dead. We exist only as the energy of God.

Picture of Bapuji inside Muktidam. Photo by John Mundahl, 2007.

317

September 28th
(The Lord's Grace)

The saints agree that the spiritual journey isn't possible without surrender to God. If we want to travel over land, we can walk. We have legs. But what if we want to fly? We need an airplane. Spiritually speaking, if we want to fly we need the wings of God. The saints call that grace. The Lord's grace becomes our plane and we fly.

Bapuji in India, circa 1965   Photo from archives of Umesh Eric Baldwin.

September 29th
(A Picture of Christ)

There isn't much idol worship in the West, but there is in India. People worship lots of statues and pictures, but once you understand how it works, you will be more open to it, because through such worship our mind receives great inspiration and strength. Yesterday, I received a picture book. It had a picture of holy Christ hanging on the cross in great agony with nails in his hands and feet. I was so overwhelmed that I had to close the book. The picture created a profound change in me. I had simply seen a picture and yet the power of the picture carried me into the past, two thousand years ago, and the life of holy Christ came alive for me.

www.everypainter paintshimself.com

319

September 30th
(Our Lives are Full of Idols)

Psychologists will have to accept the power of idol worship. This power has been studied in India since ancient times. Modern psychologists could certainly prove the ability of pictures and statues to affect our state of mind. Our lives are full of idols. Look around and see the idols people worship: cars, houses, money, clothes, sex. Then why not worship pictures and statues of God and the saints?

Saint Francis

*encounters
-with-jesus.org*

October

October 1st
(Pictures on our Money)

We print pictures on our money. The picture on a thousand dollar bill is different from the picture on a one-dollar bill, yet the value of the paper is the same. The two pieces of paper create a much different effect on people simply because of the picture and the number next to it. We have strong faith that if we present the piece of paper with one thousand dollars on it that we can purchase merchandize worth one thousand dollars. If paper with pictures and numbers on it can produce such faith in people, couldn't pictures or statues of saints produce a similar reaction? We should at least think about this.

Summer, 1977. Photo from archives of Umesh Eric Baldwn.

322

October 2nd
(Become the Wick for God's Love)

God is the guide for this world and we should join Him in His work. Whatever work the Beloved likes should become our religion, our duty. This is the essence of love. Whatever is done contrary to that is irreligious. Just as a wick burns in a lamp, so also we should become the wick for God's love.

Winter, 1978. Photo from archives of Umesh Eric Baldwin.

October 3rd
(How Can Energy Come from a Mantra?)

Mantras contain words and letter sounds arranged in a specific pattern. This pattern, when repeated, creates an energy field and has a profound effect on our mind and body. How can energy come from a mantra? When a yogi is meditating in Kundalini Yoga and his prana is functioning in the vidsuddhakhya chakra, the throat chakra, mantras flow automatically, spontaneously. Such a mantra is not planned or designed or created by man, but given by the Lord, Himself, and is extremely powerful.

Photo from archives of Umesh Eric Baldwin.

October 4th
(Nad)

The root of mantra is subtle sound or nad. Audible sounds, syllables, letters, words, sentences, music and language evolve from this subtle sound. Nad is derived from ether. Since nad is so subtle, the divine mantras flowing from it are also extremely subtle. So in essence, mantra means divine energy. Mantras come in three varieties: sattvic or pure, rajasic or passionate, and tamasic or inert. A sattvic mantra is the pure energy of God and makes difficult tasks easy. An entire section in the Vedic scriptures emphasizes the importance of mantras and describes ceremonies and sacrificial rites for various purposes.

Notes to Myself

October 5th
(Repeating Mantras Purifies our Mind)

Since a mantra is comprised of words and letters, it's possible to interpret the literal meaning of a mantra. However, the sound itself is as important as the meaning. Repeating the sounds purifies our mind. It also increases our ability to restrain ourselves and behave virtuously. It strengthens our mind by decreasing scattered thoughts. The increased mental clarity helps us attain the four goals of life in Sanatan Dharma: dharma, wealth, pleasure and liberation.

Bapuji in India as a young swami visiting a "Goshala," a cowshed, circa 1951 in Halol, India. Photo from archives of Umesh Eric Baldwin.

October 6th
(The Beginning of my Yoga Practice)

While trying to fall asleep one night, I sat alone in deep introspection. I was overwhelmed with self-doubt and questioned my worthiness as a seeker. I longed to see beloved Gurudev again. I missed him terribly and didn't feel like I could go on without him.

I saw nothing but my own faults, even after years of effort on the spiritual path and I was overcome by a sense of total failure.

"Divine Gurudev," I prayed in earnest. "When will my faults leave me? When will that blessed moment come when my mind and body are free of inner impurity? When will I be your true disciple? My Lord, every day I struggle with great effort to get rid of my shortcomings, yet it seems I always end up a failure. I feel so inadequate to the truth and purity which I know lie beyond. Now, more than ever, I need your favor and your blessings. Gurudev, I've struggled to the end of my strength."

I closed my eyes and let the tears run down my face. When I opened my eyes, my night lamp had gone out and the room was dark, but there was a glowing stream of light soothing my eyes. I noticed a distant shining star. The beam of light glimmered and twinkled in divine radiance from the outer reaches of space. As I looked in wonder and awe, I noticed a glowing form floating down that stream of light towards me. Then to my surprise and utter joy, Gurudev appeared standing right in front of me in his true form. I could see him clearly in the light that was glowing around his body.

I instantly fell to his holy feet.

"Don't cry, my beloved son," he said. "Don't worry. The time is now ripe for you to start practicing yoga."

The light twinkled and glowed, then faded back into the darkness of space and he was gone.

Full of inspiration, I rededicated myself to my yoga practice. For the next three months, I practiced *anulom-vilom* (alternate nostril breathing) according to the instruction I had learned from Gurudev when I was 19.

One day, I was practicing this pranayam in my room. I was seated on a mattress spread on the floor. I wasn't conscious of how many pranayams I had performed, but suddenly I got up and began to spontaneously perform various asanas (postures) and mudras (gestures with the hands). I even started dancing! I was astonished to realize that all these yogic kriyas (cleansing actions) were manifesting automatically.

I rejoiced at this dramatic new development in my spiritual life. I had never done postures before and eagerly read scriptural books on yoga. What joy when my spontaneous movements matched perfectly those in the great books of scripture!

This marked my entry into the path of yoga. I began meditating for hours and hours each day totally absorbed in the marvelous activities of my own prana. All of this, I knew, was due to my Gurudev's grace.

(*From: "A Sunrise of Joy, the Lost Darshans of Swami Kripalu," by John Mundahl. Monkfish Books, Rhinebeck, NewYork 2012.*)

October 7th
(The Yamas and Niyamas)

The water of a river flows between two banks and thus is protected. Similarly, if our life flows between the two banks of yamas and niyamas, it is also protected. These banks are religion, itself. The yamas and niyamas are the foundation of all the great religions of the world. The masters consider them to be universal codes of behavior. A religion that doesn't incorporate these disciplines can't prosper long. These commandments are truly the universal religion, the global religion. They are the religion of life. They are the life force of the spiritual seeker committed to living an active life surrounded by others in society. When we sincerely practice the yamas and niyamas we know the art of living. These principles generate skillfulness in action and through such actions we attain truth and purity. These disciplines are the heart of Sanatan Dharma, the path of eternal truth, the eternal religion

October 8th
(When the Vine of Love Flourishes)

Tolerance unites our relationships to others and fosters happiness, connection to others and spiritual growth. It fosters love between wife and husband, parents and children, brother and sister and guru and disciple. Tolerance is the soil. Dedication is the water. And love is the seed. When these three elements are properly mixed, the vine of love flourishes.

October 9th
(To Love means to be Engrossed in the Other)

To love means to be engrossed in the other. The lover doesn't think of himself, only the other. Conflict arises when concern for ourselves overwhelms our concern for those around us. Attraction turns into aversion. Love, service and dedication leave their home in our heart and migrate elsewhere. We must forgive everyone. This is tolerance and this is the spiritual path. And if necessary, we must do this many times over. Only then can happiness prosper in our personal life, family, society and nation.

www.worthytoshare.com

October 10th
(Prana Follows a Focused Mind)

Our minds are restless. This restlessness is caused by the contact of our five senses with the external world. To steady our mind, to make it more introverted, we must close the five gates of our senses, even for a short time. As long as our mind isn't introverted, or focused, we can't reflect deeply on a chosen thought or activity. Once our mind becomes focused, however, prana will follow thought. This is how yogis direct prana. The basic principle is: *prana naturally follows a focused mind.* So, the yogis have some degree of control over their mind. They are able to shut out distractions coming in from the senses. Then they focus on what they want and allow prana to flow in that direction. Mind and prana are then vibrating on the same level. They are one, united. The senses then follow prana and become calm, as well. When mind is restless, prana is restless. When prana is restless, the senses are restless. So first we have to steady our mind. All the tools of Jnana, Bhakti and Karma Yoga are intended to do this.

Notes to Myself

October 11th
(Mental Purification)

Mental purification is much more difficult than physical purification. Purification of our mind occurs through right thinking. This happens when we watch our thoughts and gradually eliminate destructive thought patterns. Good thoughts take us toward God-Consciousness, our goal. To whatever extent we have good thoughts, to that extent we will be happier and more peaceful. We can then extend this happiness to others. When a flower blooms, others receive the fragrance. When a lamp is lit, others receive the light. Similarly, when we are happy, those around us receive happiness.

Bapuji in India, 1974.
Photo from archives of Umesh Eric Baldwin.

333

October 12th
(Our Daily Communications)

Our communication with others is a good yardstick of our growth. If our communication is loving, it's a sign that we are growing and that our mind is becoming purified. So, at the end of the day, reflect with awareness on your daily communications.

Photo from archives of Umesh Eric Baldwin. Summer, 1977.

October 13th
(Chanting the Name of the Lord)

Chanting the name of the Lord is the best possible sadhana for the householder. It's indescribably important and can be practiced by anyone anywhere. It will bring the first three aims of life: dharma, wealth and passion. And yet japa also brings extraordinary seekers their only aim: liberation. Since japa bestows all the yogic powers and is equally useful for the householder and the renunciate, japa is more than just japa. It's japa yoga. The scriptures say that japa is the best gate to yoga. It's called Haridwar, the gateway to the Lord. It's a mental and physical detergent that cleanses our mind and body like laundry soup cleans our clothes. To learn the complete method of mantra practice, we should obtain mantra initiation from a Guru along with proper guidance. There are three ways to do it: spoken, whispered and silent. Spoken japa is heard by others. Whispered japa is heard only by ourself. Silent japa is mental repetition while contemplating the meaning of the syllables, words and sentences.

Notes to Myself

Brahmacharya is included in both physical and mental tapas and is extremely important. Just as steam is created from water and heat, so also conservation of sensual energy combined with pranayam and a yogic lifestyle create tremendous energy. We are children of God and can connect to the power of the Godhead, just as a railroad car can connect to the power of the engine. The tool to connect us is brahmacharya. Brahmacharya, though difficult, is the most important tapas for a serious seeker. It provides the energy to drive the engine for our spiritual growth. A seeker who cannot observe brahmacharya properly cannot become truly dharmic, that is, a spiritual person.

Notes to Myself

October 15th
(The Beloved Lord is an Expensive Diamond)

Brahmacharya is absolutely necessary in life. Those unable to practice this tapas should start small, but continue to grow. Do what you can. Keep as much self-control as possible. Don't give up. *This is the tapas and it is well worth the effort.* The Beloved Lord is such an expensive diamond that no person, though rich in the eyes of the world, can buy it, and yet any person, though poor in the eyes of the world, can have it. First, you must offer your love to God. Then comes non-violence. After that, comes tapas of speech.

Notes to Myself

October 16th
(Looking for a Guru)

Hunger for spiritual growth has started in the west and many people are looking for a guru. They are searching so fast, however, that they pass by the guru fast, too. Today one guru, tomorrow another guru. Today one ashram, tomorrow another ashram. Today one yoga, tomorrow another yoga. Today one scripture, tomorrow another scripture. This isn't proper. If you want to satisfy your spiritual hunger, you will have to slow down and become more steady and still. In my ashram in India, there are always three or four guests from foreign countries. They say, "We're in search of a guru." I tell them you must visit the guru and stay awhile, be in close contact with him or her. There must be love. Then the guru will give you the knowledge. You should clearly understand that first there must be love between the guru and a disciple. Then only the knowledge can be retained. The love should be so strong that the disciple considers the guru to be God, Himself. Then the knowledge will flow.

Notes to Myself

October 17th
(RAM and OM)

When a child is born, we choose a name. When God is born in our heart, we choose a name, too. This is how Sanatan Dharma works. Ram and OM are the best names for God. Ram is God in form. OM is God in the formless. First, you use the word Ram for chanting and when that is completed, when you are one with God in form, then OM begins and you become one with the formless aspect of God. Choose whichever form of God you like best and worship that form. This worship is called puja in India. Use a statue or picture of your deity as created by artists who have studied the scriptures, since the scriptures contain descriptions of the many forms of God worshipped in India.

play.google.com

339

October 18th
(Purification)

Just as we must clean a cup before we can fill it with milk, a seeker must purify his body and mind before he can fill it with God-Consciousness. Each branch of yoga defines this purification process differently. Karma Yoga prescribes the yamas and niyamas. Bhakti Yoga prescribes various rituals and vows. Jnana Yoga prescribes the removal of intellectual layers superimposed on the light of the soul.

October 19th
(The Yamas and Niyamas)

The highest religious sects in the world have accepted the yamas and niyamas to a greater or lesser extent. Any religious sect that doesn't observe these disciplines cannot survive long. The great sage Patanjali prescribed five important disciplines: non-violence, truth, nonstealing, brahmacharya and non-attachment. He advised everyone to observe these basic practices. These universal humanitarian disciplines benefit the entire world and are of primary importance for traveling both the Pravritti and Nivritti paths. (The householder path and the path of renunciation)

Yama: Self-restraint

* **Ahimsa:** to not harm; kindness, compassion; love for all
* **Satyam:** truthfulness
* **Asteya:** to not steal
* **Brahmacharya:** chastity; sexual purity
* **Aparigraha:** renunciation, non-avariciousness, freedom from desires

Niyama: Precepts

* **Saucha:** internal and external purity; cleanliness; integrity
* **Santosha:** contentment; satisfaction; joy
* **Tapas:** austerity; penance
* **Svadhyaya:** study of religious books and repetition of mantras
* **Ishvara-Pranidhana:** Self-remembering; worship of Divinity and self-surrender

www.yogainthemorning.com

341

October 20th
(The Spiritual Battle)

There are two ways to fight the spiritual battle: one is from within a closed fort. This is the path of renunciation. The other is on an open battlefield. This is the path of the householder. Either way, we must fight. The five most powerful enemies of yoga, or union with God, are violence, deceit, stealing, sensual indulgence and attachment. They obstruct everyone traveling on the path to the Lord. Conversely, the five most powerful friends of yoga are non-violence, truth, non-stealing, sensual restraint and non-attachment. Their protection enables our sadhana to succeed.

Bapuji meditating as a young man. From: "A Sunrise of Joy, the Lost Darshans of Swami Kripalu," by John Mundahl. Monkfish Books. Rhinebeck, New York 2012.

October 21st
(The Light of Truth)

Spiritual masters who have realized the truth and lived according to this definition eventually feel that the whole world is their family. Since these saints have dropped all ego, the Lord inspires their thoughts, speech and actions. Such people, totally free, have no reason to speak less than the full truth. Please remember, however, that this stage culminates after a long period of practicing truth in speech. Such masters come to us carrying a brilliant lamp that disperses the darkness of untruth. Just as an owl cannot tolerate the light of day, some people cannot tolerate the light of truth.

Notes to Myself

Photo from archives of Umesh Eric Baldwin. Summer, 1977.

October 22nd
(Guidelines for Speech)

Truth, especially in speech, is difficult. Unless we speak truthfully, speech is only noise. We can't have harmony in our family if we aren't truthful with one another and if we can't speak truthfully to a few loved ones, how can we possibly speak truthfully in our larger social system

Lord Krishna says in the Bhagavad Gita that spiritual seekers should observe the following vows regarding speech:

1. Speak only those words that please others.

2. Before speaking, examine each word to determine if there is any bitterness or selfishness in it.

3. Whatever we say should be for the welfare of others.

4. Do not disturb anyone's mind with our speech.

5. Our statements should be full of truth.

The Manu Smriti, an Indian scripture, gives similar advice: "One should speak the truth. One should speak sweetly. One should not speak bitter truth. Nor should one speak sweet untruth, either. This is the Sanatan Dharma, the Eternal Truth."

Notes to Myself

October 23rd
(Bharat Muni and the Deer)

Once in India there was a great yogi named Bharat Muni. He was a *muni,* a yogi of a very high nature. He lived in a small hut in the forest and ate the fruit and vegetables that he gathered in the woods.

One day he came to the bank of a river. A short distance away he saw a lion chasing a deer. The deer was pregnant. She jumped into the water and swam to the opposite shore and escaped from the lion, but in the process she lost her baby.

The baby cried, but the mother ran away terrified by the lion.

Bharat Muni's heart melted. He forgot all about his morning prayers. He forgot all about his meditation time. He rushed to the side of the fawn and gently caressed the baby's head. The tiny deer looked up at Bharat Muni with beautiful, soft eyes. The eyes of a fawn are famous for their gentleness and this great yogi fell in love with the fawn.

With great tenderness, Bharat Muni picked up the fawn and brought the small deer to his hut. He fed the deer and totally took care of her and within no time he was so enchanted with the deer that he forgot about his meditation time. He spent his whole day playing with the baby and looking after it.

Soon he was talking to the deer and the deer loved it, too. She would come and sit on Bharat Muni's lap and they were both happy.

Now how can this happen? How can a great yogi like Bharat Muni who had meditated for years forget about his meditation time for a deer?

The answer is that Bharat Muni had meditated for so long that whatever he did he completely threw his mind in that direction. It didn't matter if he was eating, or gathering wood, or walking to the river, or taking care of a baby deer. Whatever he did, his mind was totally there, one pointed.

So the baby deer had become the object of his meditation now and even though he was close to mukti, which means liberation, he didn't attain liberation in that life because he had lost his focus. He was meditating on the wrong thing.

A short time later Bharat Muni left his body still saying,

"Deer, deer, come to me!"

And the Compassionate Lord allowed Bharat Muni to be born a deer in his next incarnation. This is the ending told in India. Bharat Muni went from a yogi to a deer!

From, "From The Heart of The Lotus, the Teaching stories of Swami Kripalu, by John Mundahl. Monkfish Books, Rhinebeck, NY 2008.

www.forestpeople.com

347

October 24th
(Speech is our Soul)

Thoughts and conduct are our life. Speech is our soul. For this reason, householders and renunciates alike should speak lovingly with discrimination. People like to hear sweet words free of anger, blame and bitterness just like we do. We should remember this and speak gently and remain vigilant so we don't bring bitterness and untruth into what we say.

Bapuji arriving for darshan., 1978. Photo from archives of Umesh Eric Baldwin.

October 25th
(Silence, the First Step toward Truthful Speech)

Silence is the first step toward truthful speech, since it curbs our excessive talking. This incessant flood of speech makes us prone to saying and repeating things that aren't true or have been distorted. This habit might be tolerable if it died with our bodies, but it affects us life after life and is a major cause of our suffering. The best way to curb excessive speech is to stay in seclusion. Not talking is natural, then, since no one else is around. Start with one hour, then two hours, then three hours and gradually increase your silence until you can observe silence for one day, if this is possible given your daily routine. Remember, though, the purpose of observing silence isn't merely to restrain speech, but to restrain our mind. I knew someone once who was observing silence. Someone, however, insulted him and all of a sudden he slapped the offender without uttering a single word! What good is silence, then, if it doesn't make us less reactive?

Notes to Myself

October 26th
(Getting to Know our Inner World)

Thought is subtle, unverbalized speech. Speech is the second stage in the process. We can't restrain thought by merely restraining speech. In fact, just the opposite occurs. *Silence and seclusion generate even more thoughts.* It's as if the mind speaks on behalf of the tongue and then listens to itself on behalf of the ears. Likewise, when we practice meditation, more thoughts arise. When we're engaged in external activities, our mind is absorbed in what we're doing and we aren't aware of the chaotic background of thoughts occurring at the same time. However, when we observe silence or sit for meditation, we become introspective and acutely aware of our thoughts. Thus, the more we practice silence, seclusion and meditation, the more we get to know our inner world. With practice, we progress from introspection to self-observation. This enables us to clearly see our virtues and vices. As we progress with internal purification, our virtues increase and our vices decrease.

<u>Notes to Myself</u>

October 27th
(Yoga and Boga)

Yoga includes the actions that elevate our consciousness and boga includes the actions that lower our consciousness. Yoga means purification of our body, senses, mind, intellect and ego. Boga means the opposite. So there are only two paths, yoga or boga, upward movement or downward movement. Life is perpetual motion. It doesn't stand still and neither do we. Happiness comes when we move in the direction of yoga. Pain comes when we move in the direction of boga. Please think about these things. These thoughts of mine this morning, though short, come from my heart. May we all become dharmic beings. May we all cause pain to no one.

Notes to Myself

October 28th
(The Best Way to Sing the Sacred Tunes)

The purpose of this long discussion is to teach you something about *nad,* what it is, where it comes from and what it is used for. There is an entire yoga just called Nad Yoga. A devotee can reach an exalted state just through nad. Many healings, too, happen through nad. It's extremely powerful.

When you sing and chant in kirtan, know that you are doing something very important and worthwhile. You're singing the praises of the Lord using powerful words, phrases and tunes. Your mind will be carried away and purified by doing this. It's like taking a mental bath and it's done through singing. What a beautiful way to experience God! That is why Mantra Yoga is part of Bhakti Yoga, the yoga of devotion.

Keep your eyes slightly closed and turned upward toward your forehead when you sing in kirtan. That's the best way to sing these sacred tunes.

Notes to Myself

October 29th
(Let Us Stay Together in Love)

L ove ties us together, not names. Our body may have a name, but our soul doesn't. Let us stay together in love and grow together towards God. This is my blessing. Your loving Dada.

Notes to Myself

October 30th
(The Religion of the Lord)

A single divine quality generates a host of divine qualities, just as a single vice generates a host of vices. It's okay if we can't give happiness to others, but we should never inflict pain on them. Compassion is the religion of the Lord, the religion of love and the religion of everyone.

www.flickr.com

354

October 31st
(Two Famous Mantras)

The mantra that we just chanted, *Om Namo Bhagavate Vasudevaya,* is ancient. It is one of two famous mantras found in the Purana, Srimad Bhagavad. The first one is *Shri Hare He Sharanam Mam* (Oh, Lord, I surrender to You). The second one is *Om Namo Bhagavate Vasudevaya* (I bow to you, Lord Krishna).

Mantras contain words and letter sounds arranged in a specific pattern. This pattern, when repeated, creates an energy field and has a profound effect on our mind and body. How can energy come from a mantra?

When a yogi is meditating in Kundalini Yoga and his prana is functioning in the *vidsuddhakhya chakra*, the throat chakra, mantras flow automatically, spontaneously. Such a mantra is not planned or designed or created by man, but given by the Lord, Himself, and is extremely powerful.

The root of mantra is subtle sound or *nad.* Audible sounds, syllables, letters, words, sentences, music and language evolve from this subtle sound. *Nad* is derived from ether. Since *nad* is so subtle, the divine mantras flowing from it are also extremely subtle. So in essence, mantra means *divine energy.*

Notes to Myself

355

November

November 1st
(Try to Stay Awake)

Try to stay awake. Always remember that you are a sadhak (a spiritual seeker). Perhaps you've seen the high-wire act in the circus where a man walks high above the ground on a wire. He carries an umbrella for balance and he has to walk with awareness so he doesn't fall and get hurt. As spiritual seekers, we should live and act with that same awareness. Our umbrella is the umbrella of self-control. Carry this umbrella and ask yourself often: *"Is what I am doing right now hurting me or harming me? Am I walking with balance on the high wire or am I about to fall?"*

www.entrepreneur.com

356

November 2nd
(This is Called Wakefulness)

To whatever extent we can remain calm when confronted with an agitating situation, to that extent we will progress. This is called wakefulness. We should practice wakefulness in all areas of our life. Just as there is overeating, there is also over-seeing, over-hearing and over-touching. All of our senses can be over used. Just as there is indigestion when we over-eat, there is indigestion when the other senses are overused.

www.brainbalancecenters.com

<u>Notes to Myself</u>

November 3rd
(Peace, the Goal of the Seeker)

The mind stuff of worldly people is restless due to countless desires. These fickle desires flow in separate directions and keep the person unfocused and disturbed. The individual then becomes extroverted through the five senses. The five senses then come in contact with touch, sight, sound, taste and smells, which create more desires and restlessness. In this way, peace is shattered. However, if we have only one desire, our entire mind stuff flows in just one direction, greatly increasing our strength of character and our ability to attain that desire. The more desires we have, the weaker our character and the greater our unhappiness. For this reason, spiritual seekers attempt to free themselves from *vasanas,* from material and sensual desires. Herein lies peace, the seeker's goal.

Notes to Myself

November 4th
(Dancing In Sadhana)

In the earlier stages of sadhana, the yogi's prana becomes powerful. This is called *pranothana*, the rising up, or awakening of prana. The yogi automatically stands up while meditating and begins to dance. This is called moving meditation, or meditation with movements of the body.

Concentration can be attained in different ways, not just by quietly holding one yoga posture. There is concentration in dance, too. The hands, legs and eyes may be moving in different directions, but the mind is one-pointed. Indian dance is like that. Indian dance is different from other dances. No one created it. The movements came from *pranothana*, so it is the result of yoga practice.

Music and dance are fundamental to yoga. They are so important that without them it isn't possible to achieve the highest states of yoga where all the energy is permanently brought upward. This is called *urdhvareta* and is extremely rare. Music and dance are always part of this upward movement of consciousness, this upward flow of energy.

Bapuji dancing in sadhana. 1978. Photo from archives of Umesh
Eric Baldwin.

November 5th
(Swami Vivekananda)

Today millions of people know of Swami Vivekananda. Anyone can read his biography and discourses and become acquainted with his unique personality. This is the same brilliant swami who felt useless as a young man, unable to get a job, walking alone on the streets of Calcutta penniless and poor, lying to his mother so she could eat instead of him. Did he not have greatness in him then? If Struggle had not closed the door to material success, but had given him a nice job instead, perhaps his life would have been different.

www.worldcongressofreligions2012.org

November 6th
(Don't Give Your Soul Away to Just Anyone)

Our spiritual path is our own. It is unique to us. We shouldn't try to imitate anyone. We shouldn't be like sheep that follow each other blindly. One by one sheep follow each other with their heads down, just looking at the tail and legs of the one in front of them, certain the one in the front is making all the right decisions. Eventually we may choose a spiritual teacher and try to imitate that person, but we should study their character first for a long time, and select a teacher only if we think the person is right for us, not because they have a large following. Stay alert. Guard your consciousness. Don't give your soul away to just anyone.

Photo taken by Leea Foran, 1977.

362

November 7th
(Inaction in Action)

Please understand, we must act. We must do our duties in this world, but our actions should be *dharmic*, in line with the will of God, not *adharmic*, in line with the human ego, which produces suffering. When we act from an unpurified mind, ego is the leader. It has taken control of our mind and we accrue karma. There is an actor and we are responsible for those actions. But when prana flows freely and guides everything we say and do, and not just in our meditation time, but also in our outer activity, there is no karma. There is no actor other than God. There is *inaction in action*.

Notes to Myself

November 8
(Lord Krishna, the Supreme Dancer)

In India, Lord Krishna is the supreme dancer and the supreme teacher of dance. He is recognized and celebrated by everyone as the best dancer. All of his dances, all of his movements, come from the highest states of yoga. Only the highest yogis, those who have totally finished the long yogic path, can dance this way. So another name for him in India is *Natavar*, which means the best dancer. Many times you see his picture playing his flute and dancing. This is all symbolic of his high yogic state.

When prana rises and dance happens automatically, the yogi has delightful meditations. In one of my bhajans, I describe this in a poetic way. Mother Jashoda is holding baby Krishna. Mother gives baby a playful pinch on the cheek and asks:

"Do you know how to dance?"

"Yes," baby Krishna says.

"Then dance for me, "she says. This is private, very personal. Only mother is watching. This same thing happens in sadhana. Divine Mother kundalini wakes the yogi up at the start of his meditation and pinches him playfully on the cheek and says,

"Dance for me."

Prana starts with a jolt and rises up and the yogi dances. This has happened to me over and over. Once I danced every day for six months, ten hours a day. Sometimes I became unconscious and fell down. Then I would wake up and start dancing again. This was all part of meditation, so it was more than just dance, of course. There was a purpose for it in sadhana.

Krishna playing his flute in Vrindavan. The picture is full of yogic secrets. *www.exoticindiaart.com*

November 9th
(When Dancing Happens in Sadhana)

Lord Shiva is a master performer. He is a master of music and dance. Another master of music and dance is Lord Krishna. Both of them have taught me how to dance. For many years, I danced spontaneously in my sadhana. Then it stopped. When people came to me and wanted to film me dancing, I had to tell them it's not happening anymore in my sadhana. But then a few days ago in the back of Rajeshwari, it started again. It started with a few spontaneous mudras and then all of a sudden the dancing began again, even though this time it was different. Years ago it was speedy, very quick, but this time it was slow and rhythmic.

When dancing happens spontaneously in sadhana, the nerves get intensely fatigued. A normal person would collapse after five or ten minutes, but I danced for thirty minutes even at age 65 and I wasn't tired. A few of you saw it and filmed it. Then when the dancing ended, I had trouble walking. I felt like the earth was moving, or like I was sliding over it, but I didn't tell anyone because I didn't want people to know that I was having trouble balancing myself.

Notes to Myself

Bapuji doing spontaneous mudras. Summit Station, Pennsylvania, 1978. Photo from archives of Umesh Eric Baldwin.

367

November 10th
(Sacred Pilgrimage Sites)

The glory of sacred pilgrimage sites is well known and people have taken these pilgrimages for thousands of years. If people didn't receive benefit from them, these pilgrimages would have diminished long ago. Yet, even in this modern era this hasn't happened. This is evidence enough that this activity is meaningful, not useless. Naturally, not everyone receives the same benefit from such a pilgrimage because each person differs, but everyone experiences to some degree the divine energy that exists in such a holy place and this satisfies him or her to some degree.

Hardiwar, India
spirittourism.com

November 11th
(Kundalini)

Kundalini is the root of all forms of yoga. The highest attainments of yoga cannot be accomplished without awakening the kundalini power.

There is a difference between the awakening of kundalini and the awakening of prana. The awakening of prana is called *pranothana*, the intensification of prana. It's the forerunner to the awakening of kundalini. It purifies the mind and body and prepares the yogi for the full heat of kundalini. It's an important step, but it isn't kundalini. Many people confuse *pranothana* with kundalini and think they're having kundalini experiences when they aren't.

Kundalini awakens only after a long, sustained practice of yoga asanas and pranayams. It may take 10, 15, even 20 years to accomplish this, or not at all, because the yoga aspirant needs a high Master, someone who truly knows kundalini. Only this person can safely awaken the kundalini of the disciple and guide its ascent.

www.yoga esoteric.net

369

November 12th
(The Science of the Soul)

The term "religion" is synonymous with the Science of the Self, or Soul, and all sciences are included in it. Self-knowledge can be obtained through the study of the ancient scriptures of religion. Through this study, however, we gain only indirect knowledge. When this knowledge becomes experiential, it becomes the science of the Self. It is then direct spiritual knowledge. Religion isn't just a collection of good thoughts. Religion is a collection of good thoughts combined with corresponding good conduct

Bapuji accepting flowers from children.   Summit Station, Pennsylvania, 1978. Photo from archives of Umesh Eric Baldwin.

November 13th
(Love for God is Personal)

The time I spent in the car from New York to here was extremely difficult for me. I was unable to do my sadhana and my whole body was constantly drawn into sadhana, so much so that I had to fight from going into samadhi right in the car. When you enter nirvikalpa samadhi, your mind becomes no-mind and your entire body becomes still, almost frozen, and it isn't proper to allow this to happen publicly. Love for Beloved God is a personal relationship between God and the devotee and it shouldn't be exhibited publicly.

Notes to Myself

November 14th
(Prayer)

The secret of achieving raj yog (union with truth through mental purity) is prayer. Prayer is a form of concentration or fixing the mind on a spot. In Sanskrit this is called dharana. The use of prayers results in concentration of the mind. Concentration leads to meditation or dyan. The farthest boundary of prayer is where the land of meditation begins. Raj yog consists of dharana, dhyan and samadhi. It is entered through dharana, and prayer is the secret to dharana.

www.worldinprayer.org

My prayer today is…

Bapuji arriving for darshan.   Summit Station, Pennsylvania, summer, 1978. Photo from archives of Umesh Eric Baldwin.

November 15th
(Prayer is our Telephone to God)

Great men have revealed various ways of attaining God, but all of these ways depend on prayer for success. We write letters to friends who are at a distance to express our thoughts. If we want to convey our message to them quickly, we use a telegram. If we want to reach them even faster, we use a telephone. Prayer is the telephone we use to talk to our beloved God. But there is one condition: we must disconnect ourselves from other connections. Only then does the phone ring and our beloved God rushes to answer.

dailymedit.com

Today my prayer is…

November 16th
(Prayer)

Prayers to God act as an antidote. They draw the poison from one's eyes, revenge from one's heart and bitterness from one's tongue. In this way the sadhak's (aspirant) character improves and his quest for sadhana (spiritual practice) becomes easier.

Meditating elephant in the pose of relaxation, Chitwan National Park, Nepal. Photo by Umesh Eric Baldwin.

November 17th
(The Best Prayer Comes from the Heart)

One who chants his prayers mechanically does ordinary prayer. This sort of prayer is memorized or read religiously from books. When rote prayers are done with a true heart, they become prayers of medium order. The best prayer is that which comes completely from the heart and isn't spoken but conveyed to God when the devotee is carried away by his deep love for God. When the devotee offers such mute prayers, he is in divine communion with God.

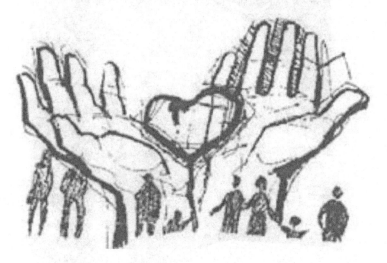

liturgy.co.nz

Today my prayer is…

Bapuji writing a message on his slate, 1979. Photo from archives of
Umesh Eric Baldwin

377

November 18th
(The Fetal Child and Yoga)

There are similarities between samadhi and the state of the human fetus in the womb. The prana of a yogi in samadhi has stabilized in the brain, so the yogi doesn't breathe or move around. The prana of the fetus has stabilized in the brain, also, so the developing child doesn't breathe or move around. The fetus appears to move around in the uterus, but it's passively moving as a result of the movement of the mother's visceral organs. Moreover, the fetal state can't be compared to either pratyahara or sleep, because these involve respiration.

The difference between the fetus in the womb and the yogi in samadhi is that the yogi's body doesn't function at all. In samadhi, the yogi's body doesn't grow new hairs or become thinner or heavier. It stays the same for even six months or a year. The fetus, on the other hand, is an integral part of the mother's body and continues to derive nourishment from it and grow.

Interestingly enough, when the human infant is delivered at birth, the child is performing *vipritkarni mudra* with the head down, legs up position. His tongue is also lodged in the pharyngeal recess at the back of the throat in *khechari mudra.* At the moment of birth, the tongue is dislodged and the infant begins to cry and breathe. In yogic terminology, this is defined as awakening to a normal state of consciousness. If the tongue is still lodged in *khechari mudra,* the infant doesn't cry and the physician lightly slaps the baby's body to dislodge the tongue and the infant begins to cry.

378

From this, we can infer that at birth we come to the waking state from samadhi. Thereafter, our mind can experience only the three states of wakefulness, dreaming and sleeping. We cannot experience the fourth state of samadhi. To experience that, we must again perform *khechari mudra* and *vipritkarni mudra.* We must make our prana and apana ascendant and steady in the head through *keval kumbhak,* the absolute retention of breath.

We must also resort to *nad,* or spontaneous chanting. Interestingly enough, crying is indeed a form of *nad,* because the final dissolution and merging of prana is dependent on *nad.* It's worth remembering here that in intrauterine life, the infant's eyes are fixed between the eyebrows. Thus, the state of the fetus in the uterus is an exact replica of the yogi steadfast in Samadhi.

Notes to Myself

November 19th
(Prayer with Affection)

Natural prayer comes when prayer is offered with affection. Through natural prayer a devotee gets nearer to God, or we may say that God comes nearer to him. When a true devotee, faced with either happiness or misery, offers his prayers full of joy or pathos to God, feeling God to be intimate, the time is ripe for true prayer. At such a moment, the feelings expressed in speech, in song or mutely, form the climax of prayer. In contrast, prayer done routinely and without affection, is unnatural.

www.prayerleader.com

Today my prayer is…

November 20th
(Keep Your Thoughts on the Lord)

As the thoughts of a lover are always on his beloved and those of a miser on his riches, so also the thoughts of the true devotee are eternally on his Lord. Thus, he is always praying. The best prayers offered at set hours are ordinary compared to the spontaneous, continuous prayers of a surrendered sadhak (aspirant).

Bapuji in India, circa 1950. Photo from archives of Umesh Eric Baldwin.

November 21st
(The Search for the Lord is Meaningless)

The search for the Lord does not entail any labor, for if God must be sought, then the theory that He is All is meaningless. If a person is at a distance, we must call him loudly. However, the great Lord is close. He only seems to be separate because of our unconsciousness.

www.heart.co.uk

Bapuji leaving darshan at the original Kripalu Yoga Ashram in Sumneytown, Pennsylvania, fall, 1977. Photo from archives of Umesh Eric Baldwin

383

November 22nd
(The Tenth Door)

The Tenth Door in Sahaj Yoga is the opening behind the soft palate. Why do we call it the tenth door? Because we have two eyes, two ears, two nostrils, one mouth, urinary opening and anus. So this opening is the tenth. It's a yogic secret. The tongue must be able to enter here and stretch up and touch the pituitary gland. This causes the nectar to flow that sustains the yogi and creates the Divine Body. It's only through kechari mudra that the Divine Body can be formed. Kechari mudra is when the frenelum under the tongue gets cut by kundalini and the tongue is stretched so that it can be long enough to stand erect and touch the pituitary gland. Then the Divine Body can start to form.

Notes to Myself

November 23rd
(The Devotee Who Couldn't Find Ram)

Once there was a devotee who searched everywhere to find Lord Ram. He cried and prayed to Lord Ram every day,

"Lord, Ram, where are you? Where are you? I want to see you. Please give me your darshan so that I may be happy."

The devotee met a saint and the saint told him, "Lord Ram is in your heart. That's where you will find him."

The devotee was pleased. He sat under a tree and closed his eyes. He looked into his heart, but he didn't see Ram. Instead he saw great beasts with awful eyes and sharp teeth. These were the beasts of lust, anger, desire, jealousy, and fear, and they were trying to eat him. He was afraid of them and quickly opened his eyes and left.

The next day he cried and prayed to Lord Ram again. "Lord, Ram, where are you? Where are you? I want to see you. Please give me your darshan so that I may be happy."

He met a second saint.

"I'm looking for Lord Ram," the devotee said. "Do you know his address?"

"Yes," the saint replied. "He lives in satsanga."

The devotee was pleased. Now he had Lord Ram's address. He attended satsanga faithfully over and over, convinced he would finally see Lord Ram. Yet, he never saw Lord Ram in satsanga, not even once. So he cried and prayed again,

"Lord, Ram, where are you? Where are you? I want to see you. Please give me your darshan so that I may be happy."

He met a third saint.

"Kind, sir," the devotee asked, tired of his search now. "I'm looking for Lord Ram. I have faithfully followed the instructions of two saints, but I haven't seen Lord Ram."

"You can't see Lord Ram because your eyes are bad," the saint said. "You need glasses."

"Is there an optician nearby?" The devotee asked. "Where can I buy the glasses I need?"

"You can only buy the glasses you need from a Guru," the saint said. "And you have to pay for them and the price is expensive."

"What is the price? The devotee asked.

"Pure character," the saint replied. "The first saint you met was correct. Ram is in your heart, but He sits behind the beasts of lust, anger, and greed. You must remove them from your heart and then you will see Ram. The second saint was also correct. Ram lives in satsanga. But your mind must be peaceful. You must purify your mind and then you will see Ram."

We are all like that sometimes. Yes, God is everywhere, but we can't see Him because our eyes are bad. We must step firmly upon the spiritual path and battle our own demons with determination and prayer and develop pure character. Pure character will bring purity to our heart, mind, and body and then we will see God.

(From: "From the Heart of the Lotus, the Teaching Stories of Swami Kripalu," by John Mundahl. Monkfish Books, Rhinebeck, New York 2008.)

November 24th
(Creating Hell in the Midst of Heaven)

A man's mind becomes like a garbage bin upon reading bad books or frequenting evil company. His mind becomes a fragrance-spreading garden of flowers when he reads good books and has virtuous friends. One who is accustomed to living in heaven and is sent to hell to atone for some sins makes a small heaven in the midst of burning hell. In the same way, if a man accustomed to living in hell is sent to heaven for some good deeds, he creates a hell for himself in the midst of heaven.

Notes to Myself

November 25th
(This is Extreme Happiness)

When one develops a sincere attraction for a real saint, good scriptures or the Lord, it is good fortune. If while occupied with these things, one feels great love for God and good thoughts gain strength, then one's good fortune is at the highest. When God takes the devotee into His fold, the good fortune and misery of the world no longer affect him. He is enfolded in a happiness, which is invaluable and indescribable---this is the extreme happiness.

Summer, 1977, at the original Kripalu Yoga Retreat in Summit Station, Pennsylvania. Photo from archives of Umesh Eric Baldwin.

November 26th
(The Divine Mother)

When kundalini first awakens it's so terrifying that it can hardly be described. Here one needs a powerful guru or you can't proceed. That's why few can travel this path. You must have a powerful guru and they are hard to find. But if you have the right guru, you can keep going and then kundalini turns loving. She's full of compassion and mercy and loves the yogi. Her outward experience may be dreadful, but her heart is full of love. Once tamed, she's like a Divine Mother, always caring for the yogi, her favorite child. She takes her little child by the hand and leads him or her to God.

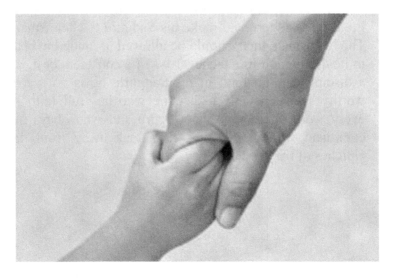

mypastmademe.com

November 27th
(Link Yourself to the Sadguru)

A railroad car cannot gather motion by itself. However, once it is joined to an engine it can travel thousands of miles because it has complete use of the power generated by the engine. The Sadguru (a Master who is Truth) with his large store of power is like an engine that pulls the good disciple to the holy feet of God. In the same way as a railroad car is connected to an engine, a disciple should link himself firmly to his Sadguru. Then he will receive the full measure of his Sadguru's divine power. A disciple should be a soldier and make his Sadguru the Commander. He should be the means of his Guru's action, giving him his soul. He should give his boat of life to his Sadguru and make his Sadguru the helmsman. The helmsman, then, should be allowed to guide the boat to its destination in whichever way he considers best. If a disciple has no faith in his Sadguru, he is not yet a worthy sadhak. Only a disciple who has full faith in every word uttered by his Sadguru and who obeys his command without question can break away from the clutches of maya (illusion).

Notes to Myself

November 28th
(Satsanga)

Satsanga is a treatise in two words. *'Sat'* means God (truth) and *'sang'* means attachment. Thus, satsanga is the means by which attachment for God is developed. If contact with an individual increases one's affinity for good and dislike for evil, then this contact may be called satsanga. If contact with another makes one's faults clear, arouses repulsion for these faults and develops an implicit liking for what is good, then this contact may be called satsanga. If the pure character of a person arouses our confidence, leads us to the path of righteousness and inspires us to lead a good life, then this companionship is satsanga. If association with an individual kindles in us the love of God, leads us to acquisition of knowledge and good conduct, and increases in us the desire to break the bonds of the senses, then this association is satsanga

Notes to Myself

391

November 29th
(Satsanga)

Good books, holy places and all that inspires devotion to God and increases abstinence and good conduct can all be termed satsanga. When satsanga is effective, one can realize one's own faults. Attraction for good deeds increases day by day. Harshness of the soul decreases. Devotion for God is performed with enthusiasm. One has the strength to observe rules and one becomes enthusiastic about taking vows. There arises love of good books and the words of saints. One experiences great joy in discussing and hearing about God. Good habits come automatically and bad habits disappear. Unless this sort of change begins to manifest, one should know that one's spiritual progress has not begun. If you find a person who arouses good feelings in you, you should regard him as your Sadguru and serve him. You must keep yourself in eternal contact with his pure soul.

Notes to Myself

November 30th
(Yogis Try to Hide Their Practice of Yoga)

Yoga and sexual enjoyment both need isolation. If lovers make an exhibition of their love, this indicates that their action is not from love, but has some base motive. Just as true lovers enjoy each other in isolation, so also yogis perform yoga with their beloved God in isolation. The sensuous man tries to conceal his adultery and the yogi tries to conceal his practice of yoga.

Notes to Myself

Bapuji leaving darshan at the original Kripalu Yoga Retreat, Summit Station, Pennsylvania, summer, 1978. Photo from archives of Umesh Eric Baldwin.

December

December 1st
(Tapas Arises from Knowledge)

Sometimes spiritual practices are undertaken which are hard on the body. People are often attracted toward such penances, but in a tortured state a seeker is not able to concentrate on God. Both mental and physical hardships are barriers to tapas (spiritual practices). A real sadhak does not consider his body and soul as his enemies and torture them, nor does he regard them as his friends and spoil them. Some sadhaks show indifference toward mental and physical hardships. Such sadhaks regard body and soul as enemies and fight to suppress them. As a result, the body is uncomfortable and the soul is agitated. These conditions do not promote good concentration and meditation on God. Such fanatical sadhaks are obstinate, while the spiritual sadhak is a seeker of truth. Such puritanical suppression arises from ignorance, while tapas arises from knowledge. A third type is passionate or worldly penance. It is a mixture of ignorance and knowledge.

December 2nd
(A Woman Remembers Her Son)

Once a young woman came crying to me.

"My son has died," she sobbed. "He was only five years old."

I could do nothing except let her cry. She was in great pain. It was her only child.

When she returned home, she gathered all of her son's things and put them in a chest, all of his clothes and toys.

One year went by. Two years went by. Three years went by.

Then one day she was looking for something and she accidentally opened the chest. There in front of her were the tiny shoes of her son, his tiny socks, his tiny shirts, his tiny cap, and all the toys she had given him.

She picked up the toys and remembered each one, when she had given the toy and for what occasion. And she looked at the pictures again, when her son was born and each year of his short life, and she saw him smiling in the pictures and saw him in her arms again, and she was overwhelmed and began crying and held the pictures to her chest as if she was holding him again. Her son came to life in her heart when she saw all of these things.

Many people in India have this much devotion for God. Their chosen form of God isn't just a statue of stone; the statue opens their heart and their devotion becomes a form of meditation and it purifies their mind.

December 3rd
(The Sight of a Saint)

A s water quenches thirst and food quenches hunger, so the sight of a saint quells evil thoughts, and remembrance of God calms down misery. Evil thoughts come from two sources: physical illness and bad social atmosphere. Since the body is linked with the mind, a diseased body taints the mind and a diseased mind taints the body. A saint is an ocean of good thoughts. As merging into the sea purifies a foul sewer, so the evil mind is cleansed by meeting a saint. As sour whey makes a rusty vessel shine, so the good habits and pure thoughts of a saint polish the tarnish from the mind of a worldly person.

Photo from
archives of
Umesh Eric
Baldwin. 1978

December 4th
(Disturbance in the Mind is caused by Desires)

When there is a strong breeze, the leaves of an oak tree rustle wildly, but once the breeze dies out, the leaves are still. Disturbance in the mind is caused by desires. When these desires gain strength, the mind becomes more disturbed. At such times, resort to repeating the name of God. This returns peace to the mind. When the mind is in full storm, the individual with faith will gain peace by saying God's name.

Bapuji arriving for darshan at the original Kripalu Yoga Ashram in Sumneytown, Pennsylvania, Summer, 1977. Photo from archives of Umesh Eric Baldwin.

398

December 5th
(When Faith Is Kindled In Our Heart)

Fanciful thoughts that flow from one state to another are like ripples in still water. Strong thoughts that last for months and years are like giant ocean waves. Powerful thoughts that last until death are like great waterfalls. These are called faith. The torch of faith may flicker in hard times, but it never goes out. Faith leads one onto the path of knowledge and action. When faith is kindled in our heart, enthusiasm, self-control, ability to work, concentration, patience, sacrifice and service follow naturally. Faith is God's greatest boon (gift). Distrust leads to ignorance and lethargy, and their progeny are despair, impatience and selfishness. The person who cannot persist at a task is without faith.

Bapuji in India. Celebration of his 60th birthday. January, 1974. Photo by Umesh Eric Baldwin.

December 6th
(Tasks Taken up by Great People)

If only ordinary effort, patience, power and knowledge are brought to bear in a task, then the result will be ordinary. The tasks taken up by great people call for extraordinary effort, patience, power and knowledge. To lead a prosperous life, the necessary virtues are confidence, knowledge, unrelenting effort, deep faith, great fondness for the task at hand and patience. Only after laboring to achieve worthiness can one achieve high goals.

Notes to Myself

December 7th
(Kundalini, The Root of all Yoga)

In India, yoga is simply called *yoga*, free of any adjective, because everyone knows the word encompassed all branches of yoga: bhakti yoga, jnana yoga, karma yoga, raja yoga, laya yoga, mantra yoga, nad yoga. All of these branches are simply called *yoga* in India.

And yet, Kundalini Yoga is the root of them all, because everything that happens in Kundalini Yoga comes to the yogi automatically, free of his own will, driven by the kundalini power. So, the yogi feels that whatever happens to him in sadhana comes from God. All the sounds. All the mantras. All the postures. All the mudras. All the pranayamas. All the various ways to meditate, and so forth. All of these are kundalini driven experiences and they become the various types of yoga.

Notes to Myself

December 8th
(Neither Virtue or Vice are Fond of Fame)

Neither virtue nor vice are fond of fame. They both prefer solitude.

Bapuji in Kayavarohan, India. 1973. Photo from by Umesh Eric Baldwin.

December 9th
(Singing Holy Songs)

Singing holy songs is a way to develop faith and devotion to God. We are trying to see God and when we sing holy songs both our mind and heart cooperate with our body towards this end. Holy songs bring intimacy with God and lets us transcend maya (illusion). Technically speaking, any action that results in mental and physical purification is bhajan. We can only be steady in satvaguna (peace) if mental and physical purification has taken place. Only when satvaguna is achieved are faith, devotion and clear reasoning possible. Only in satvaguna do the physical organs of the body work smoothly with our mind.

Notes to Myself

December 10th
(The Path of Yoga is Worth Knowing)

Because the science of yoga is useful to humanity, it is worth knowing. Knowledge of yogic science makes the spiritual path easier. Yoga is a gift for one who has faith in God. Through yoga one's faith increases greatly and one becomes the ideal religious person. But even if one has no faith in God and believes only in science, the path of yoga is also blissful because yoga makes the scientist into a perfect theist.

www.bodyrenewnorthwest.com

Notes to Myself

December 11th
(Kundalini Experiences)

In this bhajan, I have related some of my kundalini experiences so that other aspirants may receive inspiration and guidance and know they are on the right path, so they can check their experiences with mine.

I talk about *nad,* or spontaneous sound. *Nad* actually starts in the first chakra, the *muladhara chakra,* but you hear it internally because the vocal chords aren't activated. The *nad* then moves upward through the chakras, but you still only hear it internally. But when it hits the throat chakra, the mouth opens, the vocal chords are activated and a burst of sound, like thunder roars from the yogi's mouth. The yogi may roar like a lion, or scream, or chant Ram, or Ram dhuns for months and months, as well as all the great mantras of India and the classical Indian tunes.

This happened to me in Malav early in my sadhana and the villagers were very tolerant and patient with me. I would do sadhana early in the morning and just holler and shout and chant Ram! Ram! Ram! so loud you could hear me all over, but they put up with it because they loved me.

Notes to Myself

405

December 12th
(How to Produce Spiritual Power)

As steam has the power to work gigantic machines, so does the sublimated sense have the power to achieve the greatest spiritual progress. To produce steam, water and fire are necessary. To produce spiritual power, pranayam and celibacy are necessary. Experiment with pranayam and celibacy for one and a quarter years. Then see if anything has been achieved. If so, you should continue. There is no doubt, though, that you will be ready to give up your whole life to the cause of yoga.

Notes to Myself

December 13th
(Sexual Desire and Yoga)

The serious sadhaks of the Jnana, Bhakti or Yoga believe that sexual desires diminish with their practice of meditation. Actually they increase, and when this happens the sadhak loses faith. He tries to understand the reasons for this, but he cannot come up with an answer that makes sense to him. The cause of the arousal of sexual desire is that the sex center is also the center of yoga. The sexual fluid is the medium in both sex and yoga. The sex urge causes the sexual fluid to descend through ejaculation and yoga causes it to ascend through sublimation (refining, vaporizing). The desire that is aroused at this stage of meditation is described in the Shrimad Bhagavad-Gita as not contrary to dharma or the law of religion. Lord Krishna says, "I am the strength of the strong, devoid of desire and passion. In beings, I am the desire that is not contrary to the law of Dharma, Oh, Arjuna." (Chapter 7, Verse 11) Moreover, the first stanza of Nangalacarana Bhagavad-Gita says, "I bow down to the Omkara (spontaneous sound, anahat nad) that has merged with the Bindu (semen) which fulfills all desires, including liberation."

Notes to Myself

407

December 14th
(Yoga is Ancient)

Yoga originated in India. For thousands of years, great souls have done their sadhanas. Thus, there has been a constant, critical evaluation of the results of yoga practice. Plenty of literature is available. Any experienced yogi is able to ponder and think deeply over his experiences. An ordinary individual, or an ordinary sadhak, can't assess correctly a perfect yogi or a good scripture. Only an advanced yogi can do this. The scriptures are valuable not because they are ancient, but because they contain the essence of the truth. It isn't easy to attain perfection. Perfect yoga is achieved after many lifetimes. Hence, yoga is divided into several major and minor branches, giving rise to many viewpoints. An ordinary sadhak isn't able to decide which of these viewpoints is the best.

www.mindfulnessmatters.ca

408

December 15th
(The Perfect Yogi)

By deep study of the best scriptures of knowledge, devotion and yoga one achieves two high principles. The first principle is that in the first stage of yogic practice, one must achieve a pure body purified by yogic fire. That is the external sign of physical purity. The second principle is that there should be total non-attachment in the second or final stage of yoga. Without the achievement of a physical body purified by yogic fire, total non-attachment doesn't take place. The perfect yogi is one who has achieved these two principles in practice. The first stage is known as *sabija samadhi*. The second and final stage is known as *nirvikalpa samadhi*.

Bapuji in India circa1970. Photo from archives of Umesh Eric Baldwin.

Bapuji teaching in the United States, summer, 1977. Photo from archives of Umesh Eric Baldwin.

410

December 16th
(Who Is a Good Disciple)

The best teacher blesses several disciples, but all of them aren't equally fit. Moreover, they don't all practice their sadhana uniformly. Also, each one's environmental circumstances differ. Due to these reasons, the results of their practice don't bear uniformity. A question may arise at this point. Who is the disciple with the unreserved blessings of his Guru and what are his feelings towards his Guru? The disciple who has the highest blessings of his Guru is the one who, in one birth or another, is able to reach his goal, who is never tempted to leave his path, who abandons materialistic gains in order to practice sadhana and makes remarkable progress. He has complete faith in his Guru's words, takes up his smallest wish and fulfills it, leaving his sadhana aside, and considers his Guru's pleasure to be his own pleasure.

Notes to Myself

December 17th
(Sahaj Yoga)

My prana is working in the area of my brain, so my head remains as hot as a boiler. That's why I'm always touching and rubbing my head. Prana is working intensely in the area of the cerebellum. And I haven't been able to keep my balance very well because the prana is working so intensely in my head. This continues both night and day, whether I'm asleep or awake. So I'm walking around wobbly in a daze like a drunk man, but it's from the nectar of love and devotion for God, not from alcohol. *Swami Kripalu, August 6th, 1980, Sumneytown, Pennsylvania.*

Notes to Myself

December 18th
(Prana and Apana)

The involuntary performance of yogic kriyas cleanses the body and mind and makes the sexual fluid sublime. Prana here is the main force. The descent of the sexual fluid is brought about by apana. Due to this, prana attracts apana to rise. This kriya continues not for two or three years, but for many years. Only a brave sadhak may tread this path which is strewn with obstructions like secret attractions toward social obligations, deep longing for miraculous powers, lack of scriptural knowledge, lack of a capable Guru, lack of faith, impatience and unsteadiness. It is said in Yoga Cudamani, "Just as a bird on a leash is pulled back to its place, so also the soul that is bound by the qualities of nature is held back by prana and apana. Prana is the ascendant function and apana is the descendant function. Thus, prana attracts apana in the upward direction and apana attracts prana downwards. Only he who experiences these natural movements of prana and apana knows yoga."

www.litairian.com

Crown - Spiritual

3rd Eye - Perception

Throat - Expression

Heart - Love

Solar Plexus - Power

Sacral - Sex

Root - Survival

413

December 19th
(If Truth Favors Us)

We should not think of propagating Truth. First we must realize Truth within ourselves. After that we must do only what Truth guides us to do. Only Truth will be our religion, our God, and our Guru. At that time we will not be 'we'---- we will be Truth itself. We will not have to pray to Truth; it will consider us its own and give commands to us. If Truth favors us, even the impossible will become possible.

Notes to Myself

Birthday celebration in the United States, January, 1978. Photo
from archives of Umesh Eric Baldwin.

December 20th
(Sahaj Yoga)

In Kundalini sadhana, japa releases prana, which then manifests as *anahat nad* (spontaneous chanting and singing) through *pranotthana* (the release of prana). The force of the yogic fire spontaneously opens the mouth of the yogi. Om and Ram flow from the mouth while the yogi simultaneously hears other subtle sounds. This *nad* sadhana continues for many years. Eventually, in the fourth stage of *sabij samadhi,* the yogi obtains the rare fortune of drinking the divine nectar.

The scriptures give this nectar many names: Ram nectar, Hari nectar, Brahma nectar, Soma nectar, Life fluid, Nectar of Immortality and Lunar nectar. In the advanced stages of nad yoga, this nectar drips down through the opening called the Tenth Door. This is the opening at the root or base of the soft palate on the roof of the mouth in the pharyngeal recess.

Why do we call this opening the tenth door? We have 2 eyes, 2 ears, 2 nostrils, 1 mouth, anus, urethra, and then this secret opening called the tenth door in yoga. The nectar secreted in the brain of the yogi drips down through this opening and nourishes the yogi. This secretion causes the yogi's body to evolve into a Divine Body and grants *ritambhara prajna,* wisdom filled with ultimate truth, as well as *apara vairagya,* supreme nonattachment.

December 21st
(The Power of Ram Chanting)

We just finished chanting a Ram dhun. Ram is truly one of the great wonders of the world. In India, it is a name for God. All of the great masters throughout the glorious spiritual history of India recommended Ram chanting. They all decided the same thing, independent of each other, that Ram is the best name for God.

Once a young man from France came to see me. He spent a few days with me and then said,

"I accept you as my Guru. Please teach me yoga."

"I don't teach anyone anymore," I said.

"You won't teach me because I'm not from India," he said. "Is that why?"

I felt bad when I heard this. That thought wasn't in my mind at all.

"No," I said. "It's not like that. Your nationality doesn't matter to me. The knowledge of yoga belongs to the world."

"Then teach me Sahaj Yoga (Kundalini yoga)," he said. "I've traveled all over India and stayed in various ashrams and I know a little bit about it."

"Then show me what you know," I said, and he demonstrated a few things to me. Then I taught him some of the important breathing techniques, postures and mudras and said,

"Now I want you to chant Ram."

417

"Please forgive me," he said, "If you don't mind, I would rather chant a word I know, something from my own language."

"That's fine," I said. "You select a word from your own language and chant that word for awhile."

A few days later, he returned and asked me for shaktipat initiation. I rarely give this initiation. In my opinion, the initiation should only be given to a highly prepared and qualified seeker, someone with the essential purity, and I didn't feel that he was ready for this. And yet, I thought that he would be hurt if I didn't give him this initiation, that he would think I was prejudiced against foreigners. So I gave him shaktipat initiation.

Fifteen days passed and one day he started chanting Ram. I didn't say anything. One month passed and he continued to chant Ram every day, spontaneously, for two hours a day. Then I called him to me.

"Are you chanting Ram now?" I asked innocently.

He burst into tears and touched my feet.

"Yes," he said. "I'm chanting Ram now. Ram is in every cell of my body. I can't get rid of it. Ram! Ram! Ram! That's all I chant now. I'm sorry I disrespected you
when you first asked me to chant Ram."

Ram is for everyone, Indian and non-Indian. It knows no nationality. This is because when prana intensifies through shaktipat and rises up into the throat chakra, the mouth opens and Ram chanting begins. This is an important milestone in yoga. It means the seeker

418

has found the right direction. So everyone in India chants Ram and Ram is coming here now because India has found America. (*From:* *"The Swami Kripalu Reader, Selected Works from a Yogic Master," by John Mundahl. CreateSpace. 2014*)

Notes to Myself

December 22nd
(The Six Vices)

Water's heaviness makes it descend, while steam's lightness allows it to rise. Passion, anger, greed, intoxication, attachment and enmity are the six vices of man's materialistic mind and bring about his downfall. Man will only attain sublimination when he overcomes these six vices.

Notes to Myself

December 23rd
(Saints Turn a Deaf Ear to Praise)

P raise makes an individual proud and careless. The same censure that makes a courteous man humble and careful, makes a rude man jealous and cruel. Bitter censure is the remedy for faults, while sweet praise destroys virtues. Saints turn a deaf ear to praise from admirers, but give a willing ear to the censure of slanderers. They regard the censure as nectar and preserve it forever in the jars of their memory and always sip it. Faults which have not been found even after deep introspection are revealed by the words of slanderers and float up like butter to the top of whey. Thus, a slanderer reveals the faults which one tries to conceal from society. If after listening to his own censure, an individual does not take stock of his soul, nor try to get rid of his bad habits, he cannot participate in spiritual devotion. An individual who cannot do without praise as a railway carriage cannot do without an engine is like a cripple who cannot walk without crutches. The inspiring praise of a sincere well-wishing admirer helps an individual to progress, but the praise of the self-serving false admirer only makes him intoxicated

Notes to Myself

December 24th
(Christ Never forgot That He Was the Son of God)

C hrist was, in fact, the Son of God. Every human being is a son of God, but few realize this fact. And even when the realization dawns, most of them forget it in the next moment. Christ never forgot, even for a moment, that he was the Son of God. This was the source of his uniqueness. When one has such a strong realization, how can it be denied that he is a Son of God?

dreamatico.com

Notes to Myself

December 25th
(Christmas, 1977, Sumneytown, Pennyslvania)

My Beloved Children,
I'm very glad to be with you on the celebration of holy Christ's birth. Just as everyone has an equal right to God, everyone has an equal right to the messenger of God, so I, too, may enjoy Christmas then even though I am a guest of Christianity.

The great masters may be born in an unknown place, but their life doesn't pass in unknown darkness. They always live in light. Holy Christ is one of the great light bearers of the world. He was really born unknown. His parents, Joseph and Mary, were visiting Bethlehem in order to register their names for a census. When they arrived at the Inn, it was filled and they couldn't find a room.

"I need a secluded place," Mary told Joseph. "It is time to deliver."

Joseph found a place and Mary gave birth to Christ. She wrapped baby Christ in warm clothes and placed him in the manger. Only Joseph, Mary and a few others knew of Christ's birth and yet today, two thousand years later, his birth is celebrated by millions of people. This is because he was the light. He lived the light and came to spread the light and even today he is still radiating that light.

The prophet Isaiah wrote in his book,
"Prepare the way for the Lord. Make it straight. Clean it and decorate it."

He said this many years ago and yet his message reverberates in the hearts of Christians everywhere as they prepare their inner consciousness for the auspicious coming of Christ.

Holy Christ gave great importance to righteousness and self-control.

"Be ye holy," he said, "Even as your Father in heaven is holy."

What does it mean to be holy? Holy means to be pure in body and mind. We can't enter the kingdom of God with impure thoughts and actions. Malice, cunning, hypocrisy, jealousy, criticism and adultery are destructive. We have to replace them with honesty, simplicity, love, patience, tolerance and sensual restraint. *This is the sadhana, the work of the seeker. Accept it joyfully.*

In honor of the birth of holy Christ, plant one seed of virtue. There are many virtues, but love is the highest. Just as by lifting one flower of a garland, the whole garland is lifted, so also, by lifting the flower of love, the whole garland of virtues comes to us.

Wherever there is love, there is God. Wherever there is love, there is peace and happiness. This is called *Vaikuntha* or heaven. Holy Christ spoke often about love. At one place he said,

"When you come to the altar and remember that there is discord between you and your brother, go first to your brother, remove the discord and return with a cheerful mind. Only then offer your gift to God."

Dharmacharya Peter (spiritual teacher) also repeated the teachings of his guru when he said,

"Love your brethren earnestly and with a pure heart."

424

The highest principle of Sanatan Dharma is *Vasudeva Kutumbakam, The Whole World is One Family.* God is the father of the whole universe. We are all brothers and sisters, then. We belong to the same family. If we cannot love others, we aren't following religion, but the illusion of religion. True religion teaches the oneness of all. If there is no unity, no love, no harmony, how can there be religion? Separation is irreligious.

We must learn to love and be patient with those close to us. Religious acts bring happiness to others and ourselves. When you are able to practice patience with family members, true religion has entered your life. The home of religion isn't in the scriptures, temples and spiritual gatherings. It's in the heart of a truly religious person. .

So, today, on the auspicious day of Christ's birth, break through the barriers preventing you from loving others. Allow a torrent of love to flow towards your loved ones freely and let them fully dive deeply into it. Our close ones are thirsty for love. If we don't offer them the cup of love, then our closed heart will become a poisoned reservoir. The nectar in our hearts is for others, not for us. Give love to your loved ones until they are fully satisfied. They will never leave you unsatisfied, as well.

Love has divine power. If we are able to truly offer love to someone even for a moment, it will transform us, too. We can acquire many things in life, but without love, our life is hardly worth living. We think if someone is breathing that they are alive, and if they aren't breathing that they are dead, but this isn't true. *Love is the breath. If love exists within us, then we are we alive. If it doesn't, we are dead.*

When the wonderful tree of love grows within us, our language, eyes and actions are transformed and those who come in contact with us feel loved. This is the best Christmas present we can give to others.

This is my message.

Holy Christ loved prayer very much. He considered prayer to be the highest form of devotion. Let us meditate silently together for a few minutes.

(Ashram residents meditate with Bapuji.)

May all be happy here.
May all be free of disease.
See the Divine everywhere.
May no one suffer.

Your Beloved Dadaguru, Bapuji.

<u>Notes to Myself</u>

Bapuji teaching in the United States. Summer, 1977. Photo from archives of Umesh Eric Baldwin.

December 26th
(Worshipping Christ as the Son of God)

I imagine that approximately fifty years after Christ passed away a miracle must have happened. Many may have spat at Lord Christ. Many may have beaten him, whipped him or slapped his face. Many may have mocked him as the "King of the Jews." Many may have thrust the crown of thorns on his head. Many may have forced him to carry his cross. Many may have cruelly driven sharp nails into his hands and feet, and many may have mocked him in various ways. In spite of it all, many of their descendants have worshipped Christ as the Son of God. It is possible today, even after 2000 years, the descendants of his adversaries are still worshipping Christ as the Son of God.

start2finish.org

428

December 27th
(My Brother and His Cigarettes)

I was raised with so much love. Even now when I think of it, my eyes fill with tears. I had one brother. He was older than me. He had a saintly character and was also an excellent musician and poet. This is a story about a disagreement I had with him once. We never fought over money or land or material possessions. Whatever was mine, was his, and he felt the same way about me. But sometimes we differed over spiritual principles.

When I became a swami my brother left home, too. After being so close growing up, we saw little of each other, then.

But I saw him once in the town of Vamli. He worshiped Lord Vishnu and I noticed that he had a bundle of Indian cigarettes on his altar.

"Why do you put cigarettes in front of God?" I asked.

"He's not helping me break the habit," he said. "And I can't break it by myself. So I'm offering the cigarettes to God and then I accept them back as His gift to me, and then I continue smoking."

"Don't you feel that this is breaking the rule of the Shastras?" I asked.

"I don't care at all about the written Shastras anymore!" He said with great anger. "I believe in the religion of love! I do what my heart says, that's all!"

"Do you believe the inner voice is always pure?" I asked. "Can you always believe it?"

He got even more angry.

"Your God may not smoke, but my God smokes! He also smokes hashish! And also drinks! Your God may become impure by these things, but my God

429

doesn't! He's the God incarnate of purity! He purifies everyone and isn't polluted by anything!"

"Brother!" I said, and I was angry now, too, "The religion of love didn't start with you! Thousands of people have followed the path of love before you were born! I'm younger than you, but I've studied the Shastras with great faith. Someone who offers the smoke of a cigarette instead of the smoke of incense to God isn't a devotee; he's an addict! By offering the cigarettes to God you're admitting defeat to your mind. One who's a slave to his mind can never become a true devotee of God!"

My older brother didn't say anything. I picked up my few things and walked away. I left town still feeling that he was insulting and weak minded.

One year went by.

Then by chance we met in Dakol. He held my feet together and cried.

"Excuse me for that day," he said.

"Excuse me, too," I said, and we both cried openly and forgave each other.

(From: "From the Heart of the Lotus, the Teaching Stories of Swami Kripalu," by John Mundahl. Monkfish Books. Rhinebeck, NewYork 2008.)

December 28th

When someone we love dies, the pain of separation is difficult to bear. Slowly after many months, as we gradually involve our mind with new activities, our suffering lightens. The only necessity is a change of thought. If we could bring about this change within a few days, we would only suffer a few days. We could say, if we don=t want to see the scenes in the west, all we have to do is turn our face to the east. How simple it appears, yet how difficult this is to accomplish.

Notes to Myself

December 29th
(Sahaj Yoga)

Only after attaining full mastery of pranayam should one attempt doing asanas along with *tribandh* (three locks), *dwibandh* (two locks) or *ekbandh* (one lock). Until one has mastery of pranayam, one should do asanas without *kumbhak* (breath retention). To breathe in is called *purak*. To retain it is called *kumbhak*. To breathe out is called *rechak*. One can do *kumbhak* following either *purak* or *rechak*. If *kumbhak* is performed after *rechak*, it is called *bahya kumbhak*. There are three *bandhas* (locks): *mulbandh, jalandhbandh* and *udiyanbandh*. Contraction of the anus after *rechak* or *purak* is *mulbandh*. This causes *apana* (expelling energy) to be reversed and thus uplifted. If one raises prana (life energy) and apana into the head and lowers one's neck until the chin presses against the chest, one has done *jalandhbandh*. This stops the flow in the sensory and motor nerves and permits flow only in the spinal chord. In *udiyanbandh,* the abdomen is contracted toward the spine after *rechak* (exhalation). This brings the life force to the *brahmarandhra* (an aperture in the crown of the head). The *tribandh* (all three locks) should not be attempted without the guidance of an expert. When one learns a posture, one is usually instructed to do *kumbhak* after *rechak* or *purak.* However, from there one should breath normally.

December 30th
(The Man Who Was Going To America)

Once there was a well-known saint in India named Swami Ram Tirtha. He lived during the time of Swami Vivikananda. He was truly a non-attached mahatma. He decided to visit America, but before he left India, a man came up to him and asked,
"Are you really going to America?"
"Yes," he said.
"Please write to me and tell me when you're returning, as I would like to see you then."
"That's fine," Swami Ram Tirtha said.
Swami Ram Tirtha left for America, just as he had planned, and stayed a long time and created many devotees. When he returned to India, the same man found him.
"You're back from America now?" The man asked.
"Yes," Swami Ram Tirtha said.
"I'm also thinking of going to the America," the man said. "How expensive is it?"
"There's no expense at all," Swami Ram Tirtha said.
"But I'm not a swami like you," the man said. "No one will give me food, money, and passage. How can I go to America without money?"
"Brother," Swami Ram Tirtha said. "You're just *thinking* about going to America, so there's no expense involved. The expense comes only when you go there."
It's the same on the spiritual path. As long as we only think about going to God, there's no expense

433

involved. The expense comes only when we decide to make the journey.

Bapuji telling stories. Guru Purnima, 1980. Summit Station, Pennsylvania. Photo from archives of Umesh Eric Baldwin.

434

December 31st
(So, I Will Leave You Now)

So, I will leave you now. My final words to you are from my heart as your Grandfather: Try to lead a pure life. Right conduct and self-control are the two feet of the Lord. They are the doors to God. Open these doors and bring them into your life. I have tried in every way to bring you happiness and joy during my time with you and if I have failed, please forgive me. I extend my blessings to you all.

May all beings be happy.
May all beings be healthy.
May all beings be prosperous.
May no one be unhappy.
Your Loving, Bapuji

Photo by Umesh Eric Baldwin. 1973, in India.

435

Ending Blessing

Pray to the Lord daily. Accept happiness and unhappiness as the grace of the Lord. The Lord keeps the sun in the sky so everyone can have heat and light, and keeps the moon in the sky so everyone can have coolness at night.

The Lord opens the flowers and allows them to bloom, and then closes and dries them up. All of these things happen by the will of the Lord, and we are His children and He loves us. He doesn't want us to suffer or to be anxious.

So rest, rest at His holy feet knowing you are cared for.

God bless you,
Your Beloved, Bapuji

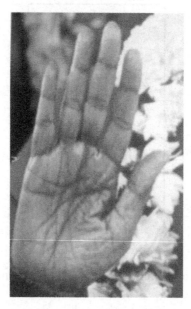

436

Saying Goodbye. September 27, 1981

(From: "A Sunrise of Joy, the Lost Darshans of Swami Kripalu," by John Mundahl. Monkfish Books, Rhinebeck, New York 2012)

Toward the end of September 1981, Yogi Desai suddenly announced that Bapuji was returning to India. We quickly sent out the news to our Kripalu family, calling all of our Kripalu Centers around the country. This was before computers, email and texting, of course, and we did our best to get the news out to as many people as possible.

It was Thursday already and the farewell darshan was scheduled for that weekend, September 27, 1981, at the Kripalu Yoga Retreat near Summit Station, Pennsylvania. Devotees would have to quickly leave their jobs and families and either drive to eastern Pennsylvania or fly to Philadelphia and rent a car.

Even with that, three hundred people filled our chapel to capacity that weekend to say goodbye to Bapuji. He had not appeared in public since Guru Purnima when he had announced that he would be going into complete seclusion, but his tender heart would not let him leave the United States without saying goodbye to us.

He entered the chapel quietly. He was thin and weak and Yogi Desai helped to steady him as he walked. He took his seat for the last time on our stage, lowered his eyes and gently raised his right hand in a blessing.

In a choked, emotion-filled voice, Yogi Desai thanked Bapuji for his stay in the United States and for giving everyone four and a quarter years of bliss. Then he said,

"Now I will read the message that Bapuji has written to all of us for this specific occasion. This is the final message from Bapuji:"

Beloved Children, Jai Bhagwan With Love,

437

I came here to America solely for the purpose of meeting you and I imagined that I would stay only for a few months. But today, four and a quarter years have passed. I have stayed longer than I anticipated. During my stay, I had the good fortune of bathing in the lake of your love and drinking its waters daily.

These four and a quarter years have passed by like four and a quarter days. I experienced great happiness from your selfless service. I consider the collective love of every one of you as the love of the Lord, Himself. For me, it has been a divine gift of love.

I have always considered Amrit as my own son. During my stay here, he never displeased me. He has loved me for many years with faith and I have also loved him deeply. His pure love is a source of satisfaction. Urmila has also served me with love. There has never been any ebb in her enthusiasm.

Today, the long and sweet dream of four and a quarter years has come to an end. On the last Guru Purnima celebration, I said that I would be going into complete seclusion. This decision is necessary for my sadhana. I beg your permission to say farewell. I belong to the Lord and I sincerely pray that I will always belong to Him.

Beloved children, do not give up virtuous conduct and self-discipline, even in the face of death. Keep unflinching faith in the holy lotus feet of the Lord and continue practicing mantra japa, bhajans, chanting His name, meditation, pranayama, postures, observing holy vows, fasting, moderation in diet, studying scripture and other disciplines.

I extend my blessings to everyone,
Your Loving Dada,
Bapuji

Everyone went up two by two, then, to receive Bapuji's final blessing. I, too, went up and placed a yellow rose at his holy feet. Then I returned to my place on the rust-colored carpet and quietly sobbed.

As I did, however, my eyes got heavy and I thought I was going to fall asleep. No matter how hard I tried, I couldn't keep them open, but I didn't fall asleep. Instead, my senses turned inward, like searchlights reversing themselves, and I went into deep meditation. In my meditation, Bapuji floated over to me in a ball of light. He tapped me on the chest and my body shattered into a thousand pieces, like broken glass, and fell to the ground. Everything about me lie in ruin...my body, my name, my sexual identity, my chronological age, my college degrees, my childhood memories, my failed marriage...the entire contents of my mind was shattered and gone. Then I was aware that I was watching all of this, so I thought: *If all of that isn't me, then who am I?*

"This is who you are!" Bapuji said, and he touched me again, this time on the forehead. Immediately there was an explosion of light inside my forehead and great waves of bliss rushed through me in ecstatic joy. My eyes opened and the room, too, was full of brilliant light, billions of particles of beautiful light all self-luminous, like sunlight on freshly fallen snow, yet none of them hurt my eyes. Everything was intensely fresh and alive and I felt like I had just woke up from a dull, blubber-like, dream.

A bolt of energy shot up my spine and my spine adjusted itself making popping noises. Then it became perfectly straight, as if held up by a steel rod. My head suddenly swirled around and around and then stopped and rested perfectly balanced on top of my shoulders.

Then someone behind me sneezed and I realized that I had 360-degree vision. I could clearly see the person without turning around. He was a young man, one of the ashram

439

residents, and he had fall allergies. There were specks that looked like pepper up into his throat and nose and they were causing him great discomfort.

I casually turned around, as if I were adjusting my neck, and looked at him. The particles of light in the room followed my focus and *Whoooooshed* over to him at great speed and dissolved the pepper and instantly he stopped coughing.

I looked at the touching scene before me, then, and everything looked like condensed light…the people coming up to Bapuji two by two on their knees crying like children, Bapuji sitting peacefully with his right hand raised in a blessing…and I knew, not with my mind, but with my heart and every cell of my being, that love existed, that love, in fact, was all that really existed, that love was the final reality, the only reality, the one indestructible thing that remained after everything else had passed away.

When the darshan ended, I went outside and joined the crowd around the burgundy Chrysler that would take Bapuji back to his residence. He was smiling and patiently accepting flowers. Everyone was straining, leaning forward, to see him one last time. People were clapping and dancing and singing his name.

Then the burgundy Chrysler pulled away and people threw flowers all over his car and he was gone.

****

Three months later, on Tuesday, the 29th of December, 1981, at approximately 6:10 PM in Ahmedabad, Gujarat, India, His Holiness Swami Shri Kripalvananda, Bapuji, entered Maha Samadhi, the death of a great yogi, leaving his physical body and this earth.

On the final day of his life, still striving for the Divine Body and too weak to sit up, he asked Swami Vinit Muni to help him sit up so he could meditate. Shortly thereafter, he began rapid breathing and left his body.

His body was washed and brought to the temple in Kayavarohan for his last darshan with Dadaji. From there it was taken to Malav, placed on a bed of flowers and buried by the villagers who loved him.

He left behind a legacy of his love and teachings. This world and our lives will not be emptier because he left it, but fuller, richer and more blessed because he truly lived in it.

Bapuji's burial site in Malav, India
Photo by Eric Banter

Credits

1. All quotes used in this book are from my books, "From the Heart of the Lotus, the Teaching Stories of Swami Kripalu," Monkfish Books, Rhinebeck, New York 2008. "A Sunrise of Joy, the Lost Darshans of Swami Kripalu," Monkfish Books, Rhinebeck, New York 2012. and, "The Swami Kripalu Reader, Selected Works from a Yogic Master," Createspace 2014. The information from those books originally came from the archives of the Kripalu Center in Lennox, Massachusetts, and was used with permission.

2. The majority of the photos in this book are from the archives of Umesh Eric Baldwin and used with permission.

3. Every time I used a picture off the Internet I tried to find if there were copyright restrictions on the picture. As there are millions of pictures on the Internet, this was, at times, tedious and difficult. To the best of my knowledge, there are no copyright restrictions on the pictures that I used for this book. If I made a mistake, it was unintentional. Please contact me and I will remove the picture.

4. This book was published using Createspace, a free service of Amazon.com. The minimum price was set by Createspace. I then added $1.50 to this price. This is my royalty for each book. I donate all royalties from my books on Swami Kripalu to charity as he gave everything to us free.

John Mundahl

John Mundahl was born in St. Paul, Minnesota and raised in southern Minnesota where he still maintains a small home. He graduated from St. Olaf College in Northfield, Minnesota in 1967 and joined the Peace Corps. Following his Peace Corps service, he received his MA in Teaching English as a Second Language from San Francisco State University and taught ESL for 32 years in Iran, California, New Jersey and Minneapolis.

He retired from teaching in 2007 and joined the Peace Corps again in 2012-2013 serving in Romania for 14 months where he was assigned to the Ministry of Education in Bucharest and helped to re-write the national English curriculum. In 2013-2014, he accepted his 3rd Peace Corps assignment and spent a year in Costa Rica as an English instructor in a national technical college in Nicoya, Costa Rica. In 2015-2016, he was selected to be an English

Language Fellow by the United States State Department and spent 10 months in Panama helping the country with their new Panama Bilingual Initiative.

John met Swami Kripalu in 1977 and spent four years with him at the original Kripalu Yoga Ashram and Retreat in eastern Pennsylvania. This experience changed his life and has been the foundation for many of his books.

He has been a yoga teacher and practitioner for 40 years and is also an Ayurvedic Health Care Educator. He has three grown children and four grandchildren and has spent his retirement traveling, writing and visiting family and friends.

His books include:

1. *Tales of Courage, Tales of Dreams.* Addison-Wesley. 1993.

2. *A Free People, Tracing our Hmong Roots.* Compiled and edited with Dave Moore from the Hmong Youth Cultural Awareness Project. 1994. Minneapolis Public Schools.

3. *Lao Culture.* Copyright Minneapolis Public Schools. 1995.

4. *Vietnamese Culture.* Copyright Minneapolis Public Schools. 1995.

5. *From the Heart of the Lotus, the Teaching Stories of Swami Kripalu.* Monkfish Book Publishing, Rhinebeck, New York. 2008.

6. *Soul to Soul, Poems, Prayers and Stories to End a Yoga Class.* Monkfish Book Publishing, Rhinebeck, New York. 2010.

7. *A Sunrise of Joy, the Lost Darshans of Swami Kripalu.* Red Elixier, Monkfish Book Publishing. 2012.

8. *Through the Looking Glass, Stories and Poems from the Road.* CreateSpace. 2014.

9. *The Awakening, Poems of Love and Joy for the New Earth.* CreateSpace. 2014.

10. *The Ant, the Butterfly and the Wind, a Children's Story.* CreateSpace. 2014

11. *Mastering the One-Day Fast, the Key to Health and Longevity.* CreateSpace. 2014.

12. *The Swami Kripalu Reader, Selected Works from a Yogic Master.* CreateSpace. 2014.

13. *Daybreak, Parables and Poems for the Peaceful Heart.* CreateSpace. 2015.

14. *One Year in Bucharest, a Peace Corps Memoir.* CreateSpace. 2016.

15. *The Journey Home, Daily Devotions with Swami Kripalu.* CreateSpace. 2016.

16. *English Pronunciation for Spanish-Speakers, Let's Keep it Simple.* CreateSpace. 2016

All books are available on Amazon. He can be reached at johnmundahl@yahoo.com. His website, swamikripalu.weebly.com, has MP3s of Swami Kripalu's darshans in the United States from 1977-1981. All are available as free downloads.

Umesh Eric Baldwin

(With Bapuji in India in 1973. Umesh is the young man in front farthest to the right Photo by Swami Rajarshi Muni, from the Umesh Eric Baldwin archives.)

During the late 1960's and early 70's, I was fortunate to have studied with Shanti and Amrit Desai. Because of their deep enthusiasm and love for their guru (Swami Kripalu), traveling to India was the way to go for me.

I first travelled to India in early December, 1973, to be with Swami Shri Kripalvananda Maharaja. In those days we didn't call him Bapuji. I only knew him by his formal name, Swami Kripalvananda. Even though I had not met him in person, I knew he held the key to my spiritual survival and I was certain that being aligned with him would lead me from the mundane everyday world to a world of infinite possibilities, the world of the divine. Even after 40 years, it's difficult for me to understand what my relationship exactly was with Swami Kripalu. What I do know is that he touched me and influenced my life entirely. He gave me an opportunity to uplift my life, if I have the strength and perseverance to do so. He exposed the path of yoga for what it is…the path of liberation…liberation from all pain, suffering and death for an eternity.

When I first sat in front of him in Kayavarohana, India in 1973, I didn't know what to think. Here I was half way around the world seated before this true sadhaka who had done ten to eleven hours of meditation each day, seven days a week, for twenty five years. I sat there along with four others from North America and he didn't say a word since he was in silence. He wrote on his chalk board,

"Welcome to India. You must be tired from your long journey." I wasn't tired at all, I was trying to fathom everything that was going on. I had never been with someone like him before so I was overwhelmed. Here he was sitting on a tiger skin with the tiger's mouth wide open and a sign that read,

"Jai Bhagavan, Praise God."

Nothing made sense to me, and then in an instant the entire universe opened with unimaginable energy. Losing complete control was not my normal nature, but I found myself convulsing, going around in circles, while he remained in silence. It was a completely out of this world experience. The others who were with me also had their catharsis. After we settled down, Swami Kripalu still didn't say anything. He had his arms folded across his chest and he was leaning back against the wall under the painting of his guru, Lakulisha. As I sat before him he was as bright as the sun. Eventually, we all pranāmed (bowed) to him and at the end, Rajarshi Muni, one of Swami Kripalu's renunciant sadhakas, took a group picture.

After the photo, Swami Kripalu showed us his meditation room and then walked us to the door. I was the last to leave. I turned to him and he smiled and locked the door behind me. He would now be alone in meditation.

On January 12, 1974, Rajarshi Muni told the five of us that we were going with Swami Kripalu to the village of Rajpipla to celebrate his 60th birthday. We took two cars and followed his car toward the village. Along the way we stopped at homes of his devotees. He would depart the car, receive a garland of flowers from the husband and wife, and walk inside their home where sweets were offered. After a short while, we drove to the next home and again he was given a garland along with sweets. We visited four or five homes along the way. It was a great blessing for the family to have him stop and visit their home. The love was genuine between Bapuji and the families. Not only did they love and admire him as a sincere sadhaka who was on the nivritti path to freedom, but they appreciated him as a person who was generous and gave all he could to support the local population.

We eventually arrived at Rajpipla in late afternoon and stayed for three days. During the celebrations, Swami Kripalu gave darshans, and there were singing, dancing and musical events.

Through it all, Bapuji had a wonderful sense of humor. After one of his darshan's, he and everyone walked up a flight of stairs to a second story town meeting room. I arrived late and sat in the back of the room against the wooden wall. There were approximately two hundred and fifty in attendance. Swami Kripalu was seated on a raised platform so he could see everyone in the room. He picked up his slate and just before he was about to write he looked my way. My heart dropped. I was hoping he wasn't looking at me. I didn't want another repeat of my experience in Kayavarohana in the jammed packed room.

So I said to myself, he must be looking my way but at someone else. Wrong! He pointed his finger directly at me and then to the other side of the room. I sat there bewildered as everyone looked at me. Again he pointed his finger at me and then to the other side of the room. I didn't know what he wanted. One last time, he pointed his finger at me and then to the other side of the room. Finally, Vinit Muni, another renunciant sadhaka of Swami Kripalu's said,

"Umesh, Bapuji wants you to sit with the men. You're sitting with the women." Everyone laughed, including Bapuji, and I got up and sat with the men. On the second day of his birthday celebration, I took photos of the activities. I was the only person with a camera and I felt shy taking photos of Swami Kripalu, but I did it anyway. I felt compelled. On the last day, Swami Kripalu wanted me to take photos of him in a school. We went to the classroom where he squished himself into a school chair where the table was attached to the chair. He wanted me to take photos of himself as a student so the children would be inspired to learn. When we returned to America in late January, we brought the term "Bapuji" back with us. Bapuji means "father." The "ji" on the end means "dear father." In India, he was known as Bapuji. When Bapuji visited North America from 1977-1981, I was fortunate to be on the photography department at Amrit Desai's two Ashrams. There were many photographers, so I was one among many. During that time I took photos of him in group settings and privately. Again, he had a great sense of humor, which we all loved. Sometimes I would take a photo of him and if he saw I was photographing him he would pretend to photograph me with an imaginary camera. He was like that with all the photographers...playful.

Among all his virtues, I found him to be a full-of-life human being. When he laughed his entire being would laugh. When he cried, every cell would cry. When he was in prayer, he became the prayer...he became the scripture. He was completely animate, not holding back. He was truly a walking encyclopedia of yogic experience. He was the scriptures in human form.

On December 28, 1981, my wife, Vasanti, and I were in India with Bapuji the day before he left his body. I became paralyzed, frozen with my camera. It was traumatic. He was staying in Ahemdabhad at Gordhanbhai Patel's home, a family that had been close to him since the 1950's. He was lying on the floor on a thin mattress, kept warm with blankets. Even though he was extremely thin, his body glowed from within. Vinit Muni, Vasanti, three men and I were with him. I had my camera but I couldn't take photos of him lying there, even though I was sure he would have said it was ok.

The following evening on the December 29th, 1981, at approximately 6:10 p.m. he left his body. I had the opportunity to photograph him the next day, but I couldn't bring myself to do it. I only took a few pictures during his burial, his Maha Samadhi which was on the 31st. If Vasanti had not encouraged me to take photos there would be none. His Maha Samadhi burial time was overwhelming.

Since those of us who knew Bapuji personally are getting older (some are already gone), many of us are in the process of creating a non-profit web-site in his honor. We want to keep him alive so everyone who has an interest can visit the site to be inspired and see who he was as a great sadhaka.

The web-site will be named: www.SwamiKripalvananda.org. Within the site will be hundreds of photos from India and his stay in North America. There will also be a section of his writings. This is a group endeavor, we are all participating equally. The site will be up late winter, 2016.

As of this writing there are wonderful sites dedicated to his longevity and I encourage you to view them:www.naturalmeditation.net and www.kripaluyogafoundation.org

I am glad John asked me to share and I am glad I was able to do so. Only within the last few years have I begun to grasp, to have an inkling, of who Swami Kripalu was as a sadhaka and human being.

Jai Bhagavan,
Umesh

Source: freshorigins.com